C000022771

100 WAYS TO IMPROVE YOUR HORSE'S HEALTH

SUSAN McBANE

David and Charles

This book is dedicated with grateful thanks to the memory of **TONY HALL**.
One of that rare breed of naturally talented horsemen, he made the world a much better place for horses, including mine.

A DAVID & CHARLES BOOK

First published in the UK in 2005

Copyright © Susan McBane 2005

Distributed in North America
by F&W Publications, Inc.
4700 East Galbraith Road
Cincinnati, OH 45236
1-800-289-0963

Susan McBane has asserted her right to be identified as author of this work in accordance with the Copyright, Designs and Patents Act, 1988.

All rights reserved. No part of this publication may be reproduced, stored in a retrieval system, or transmitted, in any form or by any means, electronic or mechanical, by photocopying, recording or otherwise, without prior permission in writing from the publisher.

A catalogue record for this book is available from the British Library.

ISBN 0 7153 2001 7

Horse care and riding is not without risk, and while the author and publishers have made every attempt to offer accurate and reliable information to the best of their knowledge and belief, it is presented without any guarantee. The author and publishers therefore disclaim any liability incurred in connection with using the information contained in this book.

Printed in China by SNP Leefung
for David & Charles
Brunel House   Newton Abbot   Devon

Commissioning Editor: Jane Trollope
Art Editor: Sue Cleave
Desk Editor: Louise Crathorne
Project Editor: Anne Plume
Production Director: Roger Lane

Visit our website at www.davidandcharles.co.uk

David & Charles books are available from all good bookshops; alternatively you can contact our Orderline on (0)1626 334555 or write to us at FREEPOST EX2110, David & Charles Direct, Newton Abbot, TQ12 4ZZ (no stamp required UK mainland).

Contents

Setting yourself up for success

When keeping horses, one thing is certain: if the horse is not healthy, you can't do much in the way of training, schooling, exercise or work.

Health is a subject difficult to define. We may think that feral horses are perfectly healthy, living the life that Nature intended for them, with no stresses imposed on them by us through confinement, isolation, work, artificial feeding and so on; nevertheless closer inspection may reveal something different.

Feral life is no picnic. Feral horses and ponies probably only live half or two-thirds as long as domesticated ones. It's true they have freedom, but they do have to conform strictly to herd rules, and whether they are young or old they may be kicked out of the herd, their lifeline, at any time.

Feral horses and ponies probably do not suffer from internal parasites or colic if they have generous or unlimited natural grazing, but they may attract external parasites, they may suffer a shortage of nourishment in winter at least, and a lack of shelter sometimes, and are probably at times subject to exposure, unremitting insect attacks, and injuries of various kinds inflicted by herd mates, rivals, or simply by moving over rough terrain. Dental problems also often afflict feral equines, and the main cause of death in areas where they are not preyed upon is starvation due to dental disorders that prevent them eating properly.

Domesticated horses usually live much longer than feral ones, but many have stressful and unhappy lives. They probably suffer more psychological stresses than feral horses, but of a different kind, and, as is now well accepted, this state can translate into physical disorders. Very many of the diseases and injuries suffered by domesticated horses are caused by us because the way that we manage the individual concerned is inappropriate, or because his training or work is not suitable.

There is a great deal more to horse care and management than simply the routine daily tasks and chores. To be a true horsemaster – one skilled in 'horse sense' – we need to develop a feel for what is right and wrong with a horse, the ability to 'just know' when a horse is bursting with health or is ill, or is even just a touch either side of that fine line dividing health from disease.

I do hope that this book will help less experienced owners and students to recognize and cope with health matters, and that it will also provide food for thought for the more experienced, as well as acting as a useful reference work.

Remember: not all problems, equine and human, can be solved –
but most can be improved.

Normal parameters

Develop your instinct

There is a well-worn saying in the self-promotion business, which goes like this: you never get a second chance to make a first impression. First impressions not only count, but they also stick, and they are usually accurate.

As far as your horse is concerned, your first impression of his demeanour on seeing him for the first time in the day is usually right. This does not mean that he may not change during the day, but sometimes familiarity can breed, if not contempt, then a certain degree of 'taking him for granted'.

If you go to his field or stable after not having seen him for several hours, a day, a week if you've been away, or whatever, and you get a flicker of unease or doubt, don't think that it is just your imagination: this is the sort of insight that turns horse keepers into horsemasters, and riders into horsemen. Keep your first impression in mind as you deal with your horse throughout the day, and judge his subsequent behaviour and performance by that.

The day-to-day care of a horse can very easily become a regular humdrum round of lugging buckets and haynets or sacks, skipping out, mucking out, tacking up, getting the exercising done, grooming, feeding, turning out, bringing in and so on. It is very easy to let outside pressures niggle you into rushing things, into being so anxious on some days to 'get done and be gone' that you may easily miss some small point that could, in time, turn out to be a problem and the start of something significant – or is simply a sign that something could be improved.

On a daily basis, try to get into the habit of standing back a bit and really considering your horse. Go in in the morning with open eyes and an open mind, and look at him before you make your daily checks. Do the same in the evening, or whenever you see him next, so that eventually, every time you see him you automatically ask yourself: 'Does he seem all right?' Keeping up this constant awareness should, in time, instil an almost subconscious sense of what is right and what is wrong so that, no matter how busy you are, you will not miss some slight but important sign that things aren't quite right with your horse.

This doesn't mean that you have to be constantly worrying about your horse: it is simply a matter of staying sensitive to his life force, if you like, to how he really is, and not dismissing that niggling feeling that he is not quite right – or, on the other hand, to know that he is actually bursting with health and well-being, much to your relief!

1 Learn to recognize a healthy horse

There are various outward physical and behavioural signs that can help you to know when a horse is healthy, whether he is stabled, kept out, or enjoys a mixture of the two systems.

Signs of good health

demeanour The horse should look alert but normally calm, interested in his environment, but not tense or unduly excited for no reason.

expression He should appear content, with no evidence of worry or boredom, and not feeling low or anxious.

eyes Should be bright and clear with no undue watering or discharge. The mucous membranes should be salmon pink, and not pale, yellow or bloodshot.

ears Should constantly flick towards whatever is drawing the horse's attention. He should not be shaking his head, and should show no reluctance to being handled.

muzzle The mucous membranes should be salmon pink and moist; there may be a very slight watery discharge at the nostrils.

throat There should be no sign of swollen glands.

teeth Keep an eye out for sharp or uneven teeth (evidenced by quidding, difficulty in eating, or abnormal eating habits).

feet and pasterns These should not be hot to touch. Should be on the same axis of slope, the hind slightly more upright than the fore. Hooves should be of even shape and size, with no cracks or chips. Well trimmed or shod, with the toe not over-long nor too short, and the heels not low or boxy: the heel and the wall at the toe when viewed from the side should have the same angle of slope. Sole not showing pink stains (bruises), and no discharge or foul smell from the frog.

legs Proverbially should be like iron rods, and as cold as ice. In practice, should look lean and 'dry' and be cool particularly below knee and hock. Tendons should be easily discerned, with no bony, puffy or fibrous enlargements. There should be no hard or soft thickening of tendons or ligaments, and no heat or swelling. Old scars or splints should not inhibit action

condition/bodyweight For general health a horse should be well covered and smoothly rounded, but not fat. You should be able to feel a horse or pony's ribs easily, but not see them unless he is turning or stretching away from you. Very fit horses often look thin but are actually muscled up with no spare subcutaneous (under the skin) fat. They should not have poverty lines when viewed from behind, no 'heaves line' down the bottom of the ribcage when viewed from the side, and no 'pot belly' with poor topline: this should be a smooth, undulating outline, rounded and well muscled, but not fat.

skin/coat The skin should be elastic and pliable, particularly over the ribs; if pinched up, it should fall flat within two seconds. The coat should be bright and resilient even if dirty with mud or scurf in a horse living out. There should be no bald patches, sores, unfamiliar lumps or bumps, spots, sores or scabs. Unless the horse is cold, the hair should lie flat; even in winter when it may stand up to increase the warm air layer next to the skin, it should not be stiff and dull ('staring').

mane and tail No ridges of fat on the crest, no sign of rubbing, broken hair, bald or raw patches.

action Ideally the action should be free, loose, confident and straight, the hind legs following exactly in the path of the forelegs. The strides should be even and level, with equal-sounding hoofbeats. The horse may rest a hind leg and drop a hip when resting, but never a foreleg. He should not shift his weight from foot to foot. He should appear to push along from behind, rather than haul himself forward with the forehand.

eating/drinking Should be at ease and comfortable when eating and drinking. No dropping food out of the mouth, drooling saliva, awkward head posture, uncomfortable facial expression, difficulty eating/grazing. Should drink freely, not play with water or dribble.

droppings Should pass droppings about every two hours around the clock. Dung should be in apple-sized balls that just break on hitting the ground, although grass-kept horses' droppings are looser, and also greener than the normal khaki colour of a stabled horse. Should never be very dark or very pale, reddish, brownish or yellowish. No slime, blood, undue hardness or softness or foul smell.

urine Can be clear or, more normally, slightly cloudy, and yellowish. No bad smell. A gelding should let his penis down to stale (urinate). Significant amount passed at one go, no frequent attempts to stale, dribbling or small amounts passed.

respiration Should be hard to detect, smooth and silent. Not strained when resting.

2 Learn your horse's normal vital signs

The expression 'vital signs' relates to a horse's temperature, pulse and respiration rates. These are not only reliable signs of a horse's overall general health status: they are equally reliable signs of something wrong. It should be understood that just because they are all normal, it doesn't mean that the horse is guaranteed to be perfectly healthy; but they are the usual first step in evaluating a horse's health status.

Find out your horse's normal rates

You should know your horse's normal vital signs so that you will, equally, know when something is wrong if they deviate from normal. They are affected by work, age, size, disease status and fitness status. Work increases the rates of all of them. Large animals also have lower rates than small ones, disease can increase or decrease them depending on the type of disease, and fit animals have lower rates than when they are unfit – although some experts believe that the resting pulse rate is genetically determined no matter what the horse's fitness status.

To establish your own horse's normal rates, check them once or twice a day every day for a week under the same conditions and at the same time. The horse should be relaxed and quiet, should ideally not have eaten or worked very recently, and should not be expecting to go out either to work or to the field. If he is anxious about anything, such as a missing friend, this could affect his pulse/heart rate and respiration.

temperature The normal rate for an average-sized riding horse is about 38°C or 100.4°F.
pulse About 32 to 42 beats per minute (bpm).
respiration About 8 to 16 breaths per minute, in and out counting as one breath.

How to take a horse's rates

temperature Digital thermometers are available that are easy to use, though they are not as accurate as ordinary glass ones. Your vet should be able to supply you with one. If your thermometer is the glass and mercury type, hold it by the opposite end from the bulb and shake the mercury down with a snapping motion of the wrist, until it registers well below the normal rate. Spit on the bulb or dip it in petroleum jelly and, standing behind and to the left of your horse (if you are right-handed), bring the dock sideways towards you with the four fingers of your left hand (a stronger hold than either using your thumb, or lifting the tail up) and put the bulb of the thermometer into the anus with a gentle, swivelling, side-to-side movement, pushing the thermometer well in, but leaving yourself enough to hold securely. Do not let go. Press the bulb gently against the wall of the rectum so that you don't get the lower temperature inside a ball of dung, and leave it in for the time stated on it. Gently pull it out, wipe it clean quickly, and read the temperature. Sterilize the thermometer before putting it away.

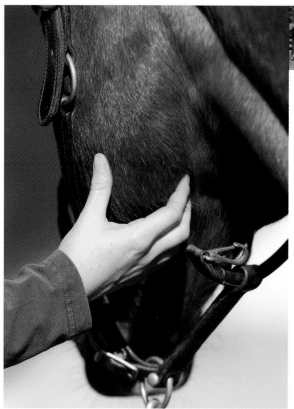

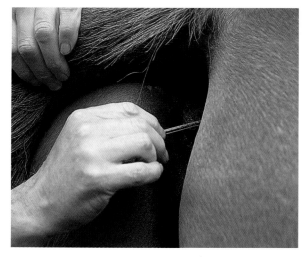

pulse This can be felt, with a little patience and practice, wherever an artery crosses a bone, such as under the jawbone, above the outer corner of the eye, inside the elbow, at the side of, or under the dock about a third of the way down, and on the arteries passing over the inside and outside of the fetlock joints. Feel around with the tips of your four fingers together and leave them in place for several seconds to give time for a pulse to occur. Use a watch with a second hand, count the beats for half a minute, and double that figure to give you the beats per minute.

respiration This is the trickiest to take because it is very often so hard to see. Stand behind and a little to the side of the horse and watch his opposite flank rise and fall. Another method is to hold the flat of your bare hand against a nostril and feel his warm breath as he breathes out (although he might stop breathing or sniff at your hand, wondering what you are doing); or you could hold up to one of his nostrils a mirror or piece of glass, and count the number of times it mists up.

TIP

Get into the habit of checking a horse's rates fairly regularly once you have established what is normal for him, and always check all three if you suspect that he is off colour.

---

3 Recognize deviations from a horse's normal signs of good health

Once you know what is normal for your individual horse, you can check his vital signs at other times, such as when he is expecting something (feed, exercise, turn-out), when he is watching something interesting (horses and people coming and going), when he is upset about something (his friend going out without him, or the vet arriving), so that you have a good picture of how much his rates can vary, particularly his pulse/heartbeat, on a daily basis in ordinary circumstances.

What should I check?

temperature A high temperature can indicate infection or a febrile disease (fever); a low temperature may indicate hypothermia or shock.

pulse A heartbeat of 60bpm or more at rest is cause for concern: it can indicate several disease conditions, and also significant pain such as in colic or laminitis. A low rate can indicate a non-febrile, debilitating condition.

respiration In temperate climates it is not normal for a healthy animal to show a rate above 20 breaths per minute, but in very cold and very hot countries, horses may show respectively very low or high rates as the body tries to retain or lose heat. High breathing rates can indicate pain, heart or respiratory disease or allergy, or other disease, particularly fever.

rolling After rolling, a horse should get up quickly and shake. Failure to do this could indicate colic, as can rolling more often than usual, or in a place or at a time when a horse would not normally roll.

behaviour Any change in a horse's normal behaviour should ring a bell in your mind. Standing away from others in the field (unless there are bullying problems) is a sure sign that a horse feels unwell, particularly if he is not grazing much. A change in appetite from normal (greedy or picky), lying down more than usual, showing little interest in his surroundings, and lethargy, are all signs to raise concern.

patchy sweating This can be a sign of pain in a horse at rest, and cold sweats can indicate fatigue or shock.

drinking The amount a horse does, or does not drink is always a good indication of his health status. Automatic drinkers with meters, or containers that have to be filled manually, are better for this purpose than others.

droppings and urine Get to know the nature of your horse's excreta, and the normal amounts. An unusual colour, a change in stance, or discomfort when eliminating, a change in amount and consistency (constipation/diarrhoea) all indicate a possible problem. Trying unsuccessfully to urinate could indicate a urinary tract infection. Blood or a bad smell in either droppings or urine is abnormal.

skin Rubbed or bald patches, and particularly raw areas, are abnormal, as are the following: broken, rubbed hair on the mane or tail, visible signs of skin parasites, swellings, scabs, spots, or broken, sore skin such as in rain rash or mud fever.

coat hair Dullness, or stiff hair (above) that does not lie flat, is a general indication of poor health.

swellings Swellings anywhere must raise suspicion. Swollen glands in the throat area and groin, and prominent, hard lymph channels that pit on pressure, are always sure signs of a problem.

legs Resting at an unusual time and for unusually long periods, or resting a leg, or undue heat in a limb or foot, can all indicate a problem. A strong digital pulse (taken at the sides of the fetlocks) can indicate foot pain, most usually laminitis. Swollen limbs or joints are a bad sign, as is frequently shifting the weight from one foot to its neighbour, or standing awkwardly.

discharge from the nostrils Any thick discharge indicates an abnormality. A white one could indicate an allergy, but yellow or greenish discharges indicate infection. Blood in the nostrils is abnormal.

injury of the back Athletic horses are very prone to injuries of the back and hindquarters. Any unusual or awkward stance or way of going, a dislike of being tacked up or mounted, a sudden dislike of jumping or a change in jumping performance (refusing, running out, galloping off or bucking on landing, kicking out with the hind feet over the jump) can all indicate pain.

teeth Dental problems can be indicated by the following: a change in eating behaviour or pattern; a new resistance to the bit; much undigested fibre passing out of the anus; holding the head awkwardly; boring off, or throwing the head up; dislike of being bridled (see below).

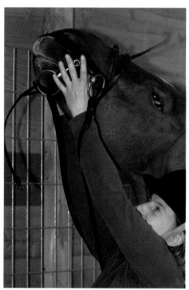

TIP

At every visit check your horse's general appearance and demeanour; check his bedding and rugs for unusual disturbance, and the walls for scrape or kick marks (these could indicate colic, or that he has been cast); check that his food and water have been eaten and drunk.

4 The importance of good conformation

Conformation is a horse's make and shape and is determined by the bony skeleton. Muscular development, or lack of it, can make a huge difference to a horse's appearance but is not classed as conformation. The horse's natural action stems from his conformation but is also dependent on his muscle use, and freedom from pain.

Neck rather short

Very compact individual with good overall balance

Rather low withers

Back maybe a little too short

Hindquarters could be slightly longer

Interested, outgoing expression

Good, open elbows

Hindlegs could stand slightly more forward but good, open stifles

Straight, strong-looking forelegs

Why is conformation important?

It is largely a matter of the distribution of energy and weight in movement and how well the body can withstand the resultant stresses. To give just three basic instances:

1 A 'crooked' leg will not experience even force from the weight of the torso above and impact with the ground below; some part of the leg will be overloaded and another will not be doing its share of weightbearing.

2 Studies show that the best showjumpers normally have long upper legs, particularly from stifle to hock, which greatly helps with the huge thrust needed to heave a half-ton horse over an obstacle.

3 A horse with a large, heavy head on the end of a long

neck will unavoidably be well on the forehand and difficult to balance and collect. Such horses will probably bear excess weight on their forelegs, which can suffer consequent stress injuries.

If a horse has good conformation overall (and they say no horse is perfect) he will find his body easy to balance and use and be unlikely to over-strain himself if he is correctly worked. Provided the trainer or rider is competent and sympathetic, he or she will find such a horse easier to school and work with than one whose failings have to be compensated for or simply tolerated.

The principles of good conformation have been established over thousands of years by the experience and observation of thoughtful, intelligent horsemen and it is

Quarters rather weak-looking and not in proportion to remainder

Strong back, barrel and loins

Good withers

Good front with well-sloped shoulder

Hindlegs rather weak with tendency to sickle hocks and, due to spacing of hind feet, possibly cow hocks

Deep through the girth allowing lung and heart room

Strong-looking forelegs with long forearms, big knees and short cannons

wise to keep to them if we want a horse to stay sound in anything more than light work. Scientists have also added their discoveries and analyses, which have often confirmed the traditional view or revealed new or refined facts.

The accompanying illustrations should give you a good, basic blueprint by which to judge conformation.

Why is action important?

The old saying 'handsome is as handsome does' is very true when it comes to horses and it can be most frustrating when you have the most stunning horse standing perfectly before you, only to find that he turns into a camel once he starts to move. It seems unbelievable that a well-conformed horse may not move well but it happens, if rarely. Conversely, a horse with uninspiring conformation can sometimes light up when asked to move and really surprise you. Normally, however, good conformation and good action go together, and vice versa.

Most horses are required for physical work and need straight action with a good reach if they are going to satisfy in this respect. They need to move from the hip and shoulder, not just from the stifle and elbow. Also, horses required for jumping must be able to jump and enjoy it!

Basically, watch a horse from the side and from in front and behind. Perfection is when the fore and hind legs move in the same plane, vertically and true, the hind legs swinging after the fore and following in their tracks, so that when you are in front of or behind a horse you can barely see the hind and fore legs respectively.

Horsemen watching a horse walk usually like to see,

from the side, the fore hoof landing well forward under the head and the hind hoof landing well in front of the print left by the fore hoof on the same side, called overtracking. These two points indicate that the horse has a naturally good reach or a 'ground-covering' stride. It should be borne in mind, though, that some horses with a longish back (as have some mares) may not overtrack a great deal or may just track up, placing the hind hooves in the prints left by the fore. In trot, horses should track up.

Any deviation from this straight and true parameter can mean that the horse may well interfere (hit himself) in action, injure himself and possibly bring himself down. He will probably not be so agile on his feet and, therefore, well balanced as a horse with straight action, which may make him prone to stumbling and falling, and a limited reach will mean that he has to work harder to cover the same ground than a horse with a longer stride, making extra energy demands on his system.

5 Understand the effects of poor conformation

Evolution created horses for regions: man created horses for purposes. Evolution, or nature, developed horses for hills, flat plains, cold, hot, wet or dry environments. Life in the wild is stressful – but working for humans can be even more so, and needs a strong, well-balanced body (and an amenable mind) suited to the work that man requires.

I don't want an Olympic horse so why is conformation important?

It depends on what you want to do with your horse. Unless he is so badly conformed that he has an actual deformity he will probably be able to perform light work even with a marked conformation fault. Some horses with significant faults succeed amazingly as performance horses, but they are exceptions.

Poor conformation puts strain on the part of the body that is affected by the pressure of work, and can create 'compensatory movement' in other parts. In other words, in order to compensate for weakness and pain or discomfort, the horse will use other muscles to try to move as required, and these are often muscles that are not designed for that purpose. This causes them to ache and either become over-developed or to be injured from over-work. If you have ever had an injured foot or leg, you may remember how you used your back muscles to try to get around whilst relieving the painful leg, and how much extra work your good leg had to do. Furthermore, the pain probably went into your neck and shoulders, too, from the tension of the extra effort. That is compensatory movement, and I am sure many horses suffer from a low level of it without their owners ever realizing it.

Badly conformed horses are often poorly balanced and uncomfortable to ride, which means that it is usually difficult to get a good result out of their efforts. Particular faults may simply prevent the horse going in the way his owner is asking – or even forcing by means of restrictive gadgets or bullying riding techniques. These never develop the right muscles but the ones in opposition, they can cause injury, and create distress and resentment in the horse.

Exercises to help improve poor conformation and action

To some extent, you can help certain faults by means of tactful and consistent exercises during work and schooling. First master the technique of working your horse from the hindquarters forwards into his bridle, which is necessary for all good riding and correct development. You'll find lots of practical help in my book *100 Ways To Improve Your Riding*.

ewe neck Do not force the horse's head down with restrictive gadgets. Teach him to stretch down by pointing to the ground, or by holding a titbit low down, and saying 'head down'. Say this from the saddle, or during groundwork, as you work him in hand, over poles or in and out of cones on the ground, exercises that make him look where he is stepping. Work up slopes with the quarters under and head stretched down on a long rein.

weak hindquarters Working up and down hills helps, as does work over raised poles, little cross-pole jumps and grids. It is essential to work your horse correctly 'from back to front' to encourage the hindquarters to tilt under and push forwards.

upright shoulders Work up and down hills develops all the riding muscles, as does paddling knee-deep in water, letting the horse lower his head. Again, pole work is invaluable, and lateral work such as leg-yield and shoulder-in helps build up and supple the shoulders. Ask the horse to lengthen and shorten his stride to encourage him to reach out, particularly up slopes. Small spread fences encourage reach.

croup high/downhill build Again, correct work, asking the hindquarters to come under and the forehand to lift, can build up muscles to balance the horse better. Work up and down hills and over poles, and perform transitions (correctly), not only from gait to gait but from short to lengthened strides and back again within a gait, particularly walk and trot.

6 Assess a horse's weight and type

We have all heard expressions concerning a horse's weight, such as 'weight-carrier', 'up to weight', heavy-, medium- and lightweight horses, a horse's bodyweight, carrying a lot of condition (which means weight – in other words, he's fat) and so on; but many people are confused as to what these really mean. Assessing a horse's weight and type is important because this will dictate how heavy a rider he can comfortably carry – that is, without risking damage to his frame and constitution – and also how much work he can be expected to do and still remain within the parameters of good health.

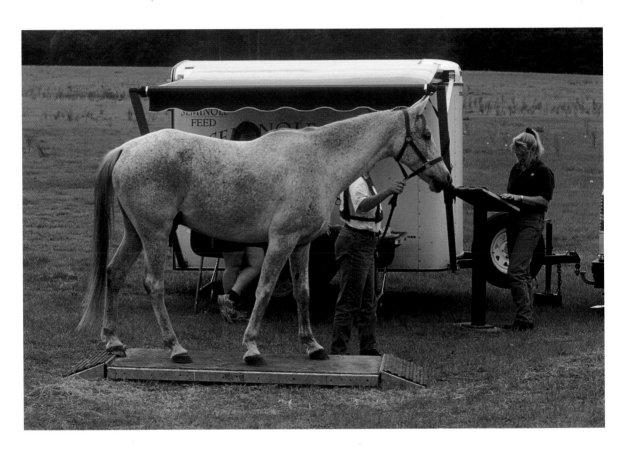

What weight and type is my horse?

The traditional showing classes with which many horse types are still informally compared are the hunter classes, namely the ridden classes for lightweight, middleweight and heavyweight types. Show hunters are good looking, with good conformation and an outgoing expression.

A hack is an elegant riding horse for a lady or a gentleman, so hack classes look for Thoroughbred or Anglo-Arab quality and even beauty. Hacks are invariably lighter than lightweight hunters, and their classes are divided by height, not weight.

Riding horse classes are for horses between hunters and hacks in type; and cobs are chunky weight-carriers, the main division being in a cob class between lightweight and heavyweight animals.

The best way to get to know all these different types is to go to good shows, particularly of county level and above, and study the entrants in the named classes. A few days of this will soon help you to be better informed, and enable you to compare your horse's type.

How much weight can my horse carry?

Apart from the above criteria based on traditional showing classes, it is generally said that, given reasonable fitness, a horse should be able to carry a sixth of his own weight with ease. Expecting him to carry a quarter of his own weight is not unreasonable -- but if your own weight is approaching a third of your horse's weight, then you've got the wrong horse! There are many who claim, with some justification, that cobs and native-type chunky ponies can carry more than these guidelines, but I personally would not expect them to carry much more.

Condition scoring

Not only should you be able to identify your horse's weight category, it is also important to know what condition he is in, in other words, whether he is overweight (fat), underweight (thin) or just right. Condition scoring (assessing body condition) is discussed on page 58, but as a guide for good, 'just right', healthy bodyweight, you should be able to feel your horse's ribs easily, but not see them.

The most accurate way to discover your horse's weight is to take him to the nearest weighbridge and weigh him – though not wearing his saddle, or with you standing on the platform as well! Otherwise the simplest way is to use a weigh-tape, as supplied by almost any feed merchant, tack shop or other equestrian supplier. Keep the tape flat and pass it round the horse's ribcage in the girth area immediately behind, or just on the withers. Keep the tape vertical, and pull it snug but not tight so that it just presses into his flesh, and do this when he breathes out; then read off his weight.

If you want an immediate answer and haven't got a weigh-tape, use a piece of string to take his girth measurement as described above, then compare the measurement with the standard tables above.

Either of the two preceding methods will give you a good enough idea of your horse's weight provided that he is in good condition, and is neither too fat nor too thin but just right.

Measurement/weight tables

Table 1 Ponies and cobs

Girth in inches	40	42.5	45	47.5	50	52.5	55	57.5
Girth in cm	101	108	114	120	127	133	140	146
Bodyweight in lb	100	172	235	296	368	430	502	562
Bodyweight in kg	45	77	104	132	164	192	234	252

Table 2 Horses

Girth in inches	55	57.5	60	62.5	65	67.5		
Girth in cm	140	146	152	159	165	171		
Bodyweight in lb	583	613	688	776	851	926		
Bodyweight in kg	240	274	307	346	380	414		
Girth in inches	70	72.5	75	77.5	80	82.5		
Girth in cm	140	146	152	159	165	171		
Bodyweight in lb	1014	1090	1165	1278	1328	1369		
Bodyweight in kg	453	486	520	570	593	611		

Tables based on work of Glushanok, Rochlitz & Skay, 1981

MEASURING 'BONE'

The expression 'bone' means the measurement of a front cannon bone mid-way between the horse's knee and his fetlock. The amount of 'bone' a horse possesses (considering that the measurement takes in the tendons, too) is a tried and tested guide as to how much weight he can carry. For instance, a lightweight hunter (not to carry more than 12st 7lb) should have 8½in of bone; a middleweight (to carry 12st 7lb to 14st) should have 8 to 9in of bone; and a heavyweight hunter (to carry 14st and over) needs 9in of bone or more. Horses with 'lighter' bone (smaller measurements), such as hacks and riding horses, are expected to carry less weight. It is always said that it is bone, not height, that carries weight, and cobs, which are smaller than hunters but with the same bone measurements, are renowned weight-carriers. Native-type ponies or, indeed, any chunky, smaller equine, can carry more weight than a finer show pony.

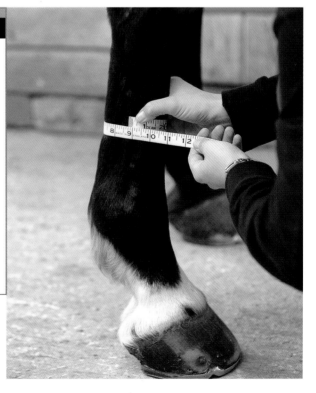

7 Assess your horse's current fitness level

Fitness is relative: a half-hour walk round the block is a significant workout for a completely soft (unfit) horse; a three-day-event cross-country course is a significant workout for a very fit event horse. The event horse would barely feel the half-hour walk, and the cross-country course would probably kill the unfit horse.

How can I tell how fit my horse is?

You can get a good idea of fitness in your horse by his reaction to work and by checking his temperature, pulse and respiration rates (known as his TPR rates).

You'll know how much work you have been giving him, and how often – light hacks round the lane, say an hour's walking and trotting most days a week; an hour or more's hacking

in walk, trot and some canter; an hour's lesson or schooling (which can be quite strenuous); or competing in riding club events, such as showing, show jumping and hunter trials, which demand respectively increasing fitness. One-day events need more fitness again, and so on. Therefore, you'll be familiar with his reaction to regular effort.

A fit horse will look toned up with a tight belly, little spare fat and good muscle development and definition; his muscles will feel resilient and 'meaty'

to the touch, not soft and flaccid; he will move easily and feel strong and energetic; he may blow (breathe heavily) after fast or strenuous work, but this will last for only a few minutes; he will not sweat much at all during his normal work; he also looks healthy with a bright eye and shiny coat, and is alert in his manner.

After warming up in walk and trot before fast work, your horse's pulse/heart rate will be about 60 to 80 bpm. You can check his rates from the saddle by leaning down and checking the pulse inside his elbow, having familiarized yourself from the ground with its position, or you can feel his heartbeat on the ribcage in the same area. After faster work the pulse rate will rise, but will noticeably have slowed down within ten minutes, and should be back to warm-up level within 20 minutes; if he is completely fit enough for the work you are doing, this could take only ten minutes. If the rate is not down to warm-up rate by 20 minutes, he is not fit enough for the work you are asking, however light or hard that work is, and you should moderate your demands. This is a most reliable guide.

The quality and rate of his respiration is also significant. You can tell if the horse is breathing heavily and deeply -- 'blowing' – or not. After very hard work, the rate can reach about 120 breaths per minute. The important pointer is its ratio to the pulse rate: usually this ratio will be 3:1 or 2:1 – that is, three or two heartbeats to one in-out breath – but if the ratio ever approaches 1:1 – that is, with the respiration and pulse nearly the same – the horse has been seriously distressed and you should call a vet.

The temperature may rise to 43°C or 106°F after peak work, though it will be less after more moderate work, of course. All rates must be back to resting rates within an hour; if they aren't, get veterinary help.

How fit does my horse need to be?

The next question must be: 'For what?' Everything depends on what work he does, and to the horse, working at his best level for his fitness is hard work.

Peak equine fitness is achieved in racehorses and endurance horses doing 100-mile rides and races. Three-day eventers and driving trials horses are next down the scale, very fit but not at peak. The next level down will comprise polo and gymkhana ponies, show jumpers, hunters, Le Trec horses and the like, then dressage horses, riding club horses, driving horses, show horses and so on; and at the lowest end of the scale, horses used for pleasure hacking that probably don't work hard at all, but just take exercise in the same degree that they would in the normal course of their existence, and often much less.

8 Develop a suitable fitness programme

Athletic fitness is necessary for all horses expected to work hard, at whatever level. This does not mean that every horse should be taken to his maximum fitness, but he does need to be fit in heart and lungs, and in his muscles and other soft tissues, if he is to work with minimal risk of injury or undue fatigue. Distressing a horse is very bad horsemastership.

What is the basic six-week programme?

the first phase The fitter you are going to need your horse, the longer you need to spend at the start on slow work, namely walking. For the first two weeks, start with half an hour for about five days a week walking on easy going – not soft or deep, as these are hard work and can stress tendons, ligaments and muscles. Do not drive the horse on and nag him, but don't let him dawdle, either. Work for two days, then rest one day, work for three days, rest one day. By the end of two weeks he should be walking out up to his bridle for about an hour and a half.

If he is required to be very fit, extend the walking to three or four weeks, so that by the end of a month he is swinging along athletically, up and down gentle hills on basically a long rein with periods of being asked, with seat, legs and voice, to come forward up to his bridle, into a feeling but gentle hand.

the second phase Now start trotting, gently at first on firm going (roads are fine if you trot at a slow to moderate speed) to 'harden up' the legs. This traditional use of roadwork was criticized a few years ago and the practice abandoned, but most people have returned to it, because in practice, it does help

Fitness for the job

Many 'pleasure' horses today do little actual work, and may be healthy but not athletically fit: many do not even have enough exercise to keep them mentally and physically toned up. Horses in this situation are said to be 'soft' – that is, completely unfit. At the other end of the scale is peak fitness such as is needed for racing and the longer endurance rides and races. You can find a fitness programme for any equestrian discipline, but first your horse must go through a basic six- or eight-week programme to get him half fit; this forms the basis for further fitness or specialization.

POINTS TO CONSIDER

In order for the heart and lungs to be stressed enough to react and grow stronger in response to work, attaining cardiovascular fitness, the pulse/heart rate (number of beats per minute) needs to be raised to 100 bpm. In an unfit horse it will take little effort to do this, but in a quite fit one it will take more work. Once the horse is quite fit, the rate needs to be raised regularly to 160 bpm for aerobic fitness, and to 200 bpm for anaerobic fitness (see pages 24 and 25). After peak effort, the rate may rise to 240 bpm. Frequently check your horse's rates, as described on pages 20 and 21.

to toughen up the horse. By the end of another two weeks, the exercise period should have reached two hours a day, five or six days a week, and the horse should be trotting out for two or three spells of ten minutes in that period.

the third phase Cantering is now introduced, gradually and in controlled fashion, and with the horse travelling well within himself. He should not be allowed, or asked, to gallop. Small jumps can be introduced, too. After another two weeks of this, the horse should be cantering easily for a quarter of an hour twice per session without any sign of distress, including up moderate hills.

The horse is now said to be half fit, and if everything has gone according to plan, he should be fit for showing, easy show-jumping or cross-country rounds, half a day's moderate hunting, up to 45 minutes schooling/instruction, and so on.

Where do we go from here?

After this you can introduce the occasional 'hand gallop' – a three-quarter speed canter – and carry on gradually stressing your horse's body until he is as fit as you need him. There are several good books on fitness to help you.

9 Understand muscle development

The horse's muscles are his 'movers and shakers', or rather 'shapers'. A knowledgeable trainer knows just by looking at a horse how he has been worked because of the shape of his body and his muscle development. Without adequately developed and maintained muscles the horse cannot work effectively and is prone to injury.

About muscles

There are various types of muscle tissue, but for work and fitness we are concerned with skeletal muscle, so called because such muscles are attached to, and move bones.

Muscles are heavy, powerful, sensitive structures well supplied with blood and nerves. They operate in opposing, complementary pairs or groups to move various parts of the body in different ways (a leg forwards and back, the neck up and down), and to control and stabilize movement. They consist of cells (muscle fibres) arranged in bundles bound together by a membrane of fibrous tissue ('connective' tissue). Each fibre is composed of smaller myofibrils (myo =

'muscle', fibril = 'little fibre'), also arranged in bound bundles within each fibre.

In response to messages from the nerves, the fibres can shorten or contract to 'work' the muscle, which eventually increases in size in response to demand and nourishment. Muscles cannot stretch themselves, but are stretched by the contraction of other muscles working in opposition to them.

A horse may have mainly aerobic muscle fibres (needing oxygen to work) or anaerobic fibres (working without oxygen). The former are suited to longer, slower work such as endurance riding, steeplechasing, cross-country, dressage and hunting, and the latter to short, sharp, fast work such as sprinting, polo, gymkhana and speed jumping. This is because during very fast (anaerobic) work, the muscles' demand for fuel and oxygen may outstrip the body's capacity to supply it. Horses always have a mixture of both types of fibre, and appropriate work and training can change the balance – but only to a certain extent.

Muscles are maintained by blood and lymph. These supply nutrients and oxygen, and clear away waste products such as carbon dioxide or, in the case of anaerobic work, lactic acid. For muscle health it is essential that stretching (rest and relaxation) frequently follows contraction (work) in an exercise/schooling session, because blood and lymph cannot pass so easily through tight, contracted muscle, therefore the fibres are not adequately serviced.

Working horses for many minutes at a time without giving them the opportunity to stretch results in poor muscle-tissue health, and can lead to injury and muscle spasm, and therefore to injured, 'muscle-bound' horses. The same applies to horses that are made to stand, sometimes for hours, in contraptions that force them 'into an outline', with no opportunity for relief from the undoubted pain and distress that this causes them. I believe that there is no quick route to achieving correct, safe posture and muscle development, and using these practices must surely be contrary to equine welfare, and raise questions as to their perpetrators' real motives.

How can I develop my horse's muscles?

Quite simply by working and feeding him correctly and sensibly. A gradually increasing fitness and strengthening programme, and a feeding regime to suit the increasing workload, always fulfils this objective as long as the horse is basically healthy.

Ideally, find a teacher experienced in several disciplines and with an accurate knowledge of exercise physiology who can help you work out a programme for achieving both athletic fitness and gymnastic strength and agility. As well as heart and lung fitness, and aerobic and anaerobic muscle function, you must school your horse gymnastically, including both strengthening and stretching work, in order to attain even, all-round muscle development, health and effective function.

To achieve this the horse must learn to go with his back and belly up, and his hindquarters tilted down so that his hind legs can reach forwards to 'push from the back'. Initially the head and neck need to stretch forwards, downwards and out; later, as the horse's muscle tone improves, he should stretch up and forwards. As a rider it is important never to haul the horse's 'front end' in and back, or to pull the muzzle behind a vertical line, as this can cause incorrect muscle development.

Once you have made a horse fit, strong and supple, you'll know where you are next time: it can be a very rewarding process.

GYMNASTIC SCHOOLING

Gymnastic schooling includes shoulder-in, shoulder-out and leg-yield, transitions, lengthening and shortening of the stride, pole work and gridwork (gymnastic jumping), and simply going correctly, as described.

10 Special healthcare for the ageing horse

Because horses are living and working longer these days, some owners may overlook the fact that their horse or pony is getting on in years and is not what he was. Ageing is a very individual thing, but there are common signs that you can look for and plenty you can do to delay the process. It's all a matter of perception, care and compromise.

How will my horse change as he ages?

Your horse may show only some of the following signs of ageing, but being aware of them will help you to know how he, individually, is responding to this inevitable process. With hot-blooded horses such as Thoroughbreds and Arabs, their spirit may keep them going so that their owner is unaware of what is happening; therefore, it is important to become very perceptive as your horse begins to age (say, from roughly 15 or 16 years of age).

- Looked at from a short distance away, an older horse may start to drop in the back, belly and fetlocks due to weakening tissues.
- His legs may become somewhat overbent at, or even back at the knee; muscle tone may be harder to maintain; and he may lose his topline despite not being thin.
- Bodyweight does drop in some animals, and gets worse if the diet is not adjusted. His appetite may change; normally it will reduce, but some horses with clinical problems in fact eat and drink more, but without being able to maintain their weight.
- In movement he may seem stiffer and less agile, he loses the spring in his step, his action may change due to old injuries and weaker tissues, and he may develop some form of arthritis that progressively disables him and causes pain and suffering. It can arise anywhere, but is apparently most common in the feet, legs and back.
- Basic wear and tear on joints will cause damaged joint cartilage, and this will affect his action, and inevitably his ability and willingness to work.
- He will almost certainly not be able to do the same amount of work, or to work as well as when he was younger, because his body systems slowly become less efficient at processing and using nutrients, and so energy production reduces.
- This may also mean that his immune system is not so efficient, and sickness and injury are not so easily overcome.

- His head may show grey hairs on the face, and the hollows will deepen above his eyes.
- His incisors (front teeth) viewed from the side will be longer and will protrude more into a V-shape. A brown line known as Galvayne's Groove usually appears at the top of the corner incisor at around ten years of age; normally this will have grown out by the age of about 30. The back or cheek teeth (pre-molars and molars) may become badly worn down, even as far as the softer roots, meaning that the horse cannot chew fibrous food efficiently.
- Any allergies that he suffers from may become worse as his immune system becomes less able to cope with them. Respiratory problems in the form of RAO (recurrent airway obstruction) – formerly called COPD (chronic obstructive pulmonary disease), broken wind or heaves – which can be progressive if not managed, may make breathing difficult for him.
- Cushing's syndrome, with associated laminitis, and also diabetes, are not uncommon in older horses and ponies.

Be aware of his changing needs

Because old horses become generally more sensitive to their environment, be aware that they will be increasingly incapable of withstanding extremes of weather: hot sun, hard ground, flies, rain, wind and cold are all really bad for them, and they must have effective shelter if they are not to suffer.

Often an old horse's personality becomes more exaggerated as he ages – if he has been affectionate all his life he may become more so, and vice versa. Remember, though, that failing health and strength can make some horses – just like people – less tolerant, more crotchety, or depressed and dull. In the field, old horses are often bullied, and suffer injuries and reduced status in the herd.

Horses often express their likes and dislikes more strongly in age, they are less able to cope with upsets and changes, and they find a reliable routine reassuring.

11 Make your old horse more comfortable

A horse that is really feeling his age, like an older person, is often less energetic, weaker, and more susceptible to stress from any source. In the main this means a reducing ability to work, and that he is increasingly incapable of withstanding the rigours of the weather. A life out at grass 'enjoying a well-earned retirement' is usually the worst thing for the old horse in all but the kindest weather.

Looking after the older horse

- He needs a complete veterinary medical examination every year, probably at the time he has his booster vaccinations. Have a full equine blood profile done to check his general health, and in order to help identify any emerging problems. The vet will check his mobility, eyes, wind and heart.
- Keep internal parasites well in check by rigorously following a worming programme worked out by your vet in the light of the horse's environment and lifestyle, and also bearing in mind emerging parasite resistances to medicines and the availability of new drugs.
- Have his teeth checked every three months. Deteriorating teeth are a common cause of severe discomfort, weight loss and worsening health in old horses.
- Condition score your horse and check his weight every week. Check and record his temperature, pulse and respiration rates at rest and after exercise.
- Be ready to give your horse softer, and maybe more concentrated feed, higher protein, a little more oil, an appropriate 'senior' supplement or special feed, and softer fibre as his ability to eat and digest food decreases. Ring the helpline at the firm whose feeds you use for free, expert advice from an equine nutritionist.
- Frequent easy work (most days of the week) keeps horses mentally and physically involved, feeling wanted, and bodily toned up. Erratic, occasional exercise is bad for them and stressful.
- Keep your horse warm in winter and cool in summer. Really effective shelter is essential all year round. Do not clip your old horse if he is in only light work. Use lightweight, warm clothing with a neck cover and tail flap, but don't muffle him up. In summer, use an insect sheet outdoors. Have turnout rugs for both cool and cold weather – wind and wet are torture to old horses.

- Keep his feet in the best possible order, whether he is shod or unshod. If the process of shoeing is uncomfortable or painful for him, give him a few days of phenylbutazone before and after the farrier's visit.
- If painkillers or other medicines are needed to keep your old horse comfortable, give them meticulously in accordance with your vet's instructions. Do not skimp on veterinary advice and care with a geriatric horse.
- All old horses need more care, not less, than when young.

HOLISTIC TIP

Complementary therapies can really help, especially herbalism, homoeopathy, magnet therapy, shiatsu and gentle massage and stretches.

12 Understand mood changes in mares and geldings

As most of us realize, horses are not zombies! They have personalities, likes and dislikes, and, like all mammals, are largely controlled by their hormones. They also have biorhythms like us – some are larks, some owls – and many are affected by the weather, working and feeling best in winter or summer accordingly.

What causes mood changes?

The most problematic mood changes are those experienced by mares when they are in season, and the answer to this question is then definitely 'hormones', and specifically oestrogen. Hormones are extremely powerful chemical messengers, whose effects are more or less irresistible. It is the rise of oestrogen to make mares amenable to mating for about five days out of every 22 or so, that can seem to change a mare's entire personality. As oestrogen levels fall again and progesterone rises, she goes out of season and resumes normal behaviour.

As well as this roughly three-week cycle in females, there is an annual cycle that affects mares, stallions and geldings: about three-quarters of geldings retain stallion characteristics. This is why, in early spring, the horse population often appears to succumb to corporate hysteria as the rising light levels that pass through the eye and are perceived by the brain bring minds and bodies into breeding condition, causing highly excitable behaviour.

Also, the irresistible smell of young grass – a horse's birthright – emerging from the winter earth causes horses to experience a rush of adrenalin, and this is perfectly understandable. Sadly for those denied grass (which I consider to be unfair treatment and bad horse management), life is now extremely frustrating.

What can I do?

As a vet friend of mine once said: 'If you can't stand mareish behaviour, buy a gelding!' Point taken. However …in any particularly difficult case, veterinary techniques could be considered which involve giving the mare synthetic hormones to stop her coming into season. In cases of extreme behaviour, ovarian cysts or other problems might be investigated; veterinary advice should certainly be taken and could be very helpful.

HOLISTIC TIP

Herbal and homoeopathic remedies are often really effective for mares during spring, summer and winter. Geldings, too, can benefit from a general herbal calmer in early spring. It is in early spring, before the hormones have settled, that most problems occur; at other times common sense, equestrian tact and patience are invaluable!

13 Suit skin care to the season

The skin is the largest organ of the body. It is elastic and cushioning, but in parts is very thin (under the belly, inside the legs and on the head particularly), being thickest over the back to protect against the weather.

What does the skin do?

It plays a major role in the following body functions:

- heat regulation;
- monitoring nervous sensations from the environment;
- excreting toxins via sweat;
- protecting against the sun and against injury, in helping to store and regulate the body's levels of water, electrolytes, proteins, vitamins and fats;
- boosting the immune system;
- generally helping to protect the body from the outside world;
- it can repair itself;
- it also forms the base for the hair roots, the sweat glands and the oil glands.

What can I do to help?

Always keep a close eye on the skin. Breaks in the skin (cuts, tears, abrasions, stings from plants or insects and so on) allow infection to get in, and attract insects.

In all seasons:

- A daily inspection, running your fingers over every square inch, will enable you to check for the presence of parasites, injuries and disease.
- Do not wash your horse with grease-destroying shampoos. Inside or out, the horse needs his natural oil. Body brushing, or using clear, warm water, are safer ways to keep the horse clean.
- Pressure on the skin from tack,

clothing, boots and bandages can actually kill skin in time: it flattens the blood vessels serving it, and creates pain, numbness and skin death. Friction causes rubbed, broken hair, also baldness, and raw, injured skin. Watch for signs such as disturbed hair or swellings. Also watch for your horse rubbing or biting himself more than a little, a sure sign that trouble is brewing.

In spring and summer:

- A major problem is sweet itch, an allergic reaction to the saliva of the culicoides midge. Protective sheets are now very effective. It may help to avoid corn/maize, lucerne/alfalfa and molasses and other sweeteners, as may adding cider vinegar and garlic to the feed, and putting a sulphur block in the water.
- Insecticides and insect repellents are numerous, but most do not live up to their claims. Check with your vet as to which are the best, or follow word-of-mouth recommendation. Natural protectors include garlic, onions and dried lavender hanging in the stable.

In autumn and winter:

- Skin becomes soft and weak when constantly wet, allowing mud fever and rain rash to develop; so keep your horse well sheltered, give him dry standing and suitable clothing.
- The horse's winter coat is flattened by clothing, so losing its warm-air layer. Unclipped horses may only need a light waterproof sheet to protect them from chilling.

14 Care before, during, and after work

Your horse's work is the main reason you keep him, but it can also be a risky time for both of you. Taking certain precautions can make things safer, more productive and more rewarding.

Before work:

- Be sure that your horse appears normal in mind and body, as working a sick horse is cruel, can make matters worse, and may cause accidents.
- Take a mobile phone, also a small first-aid kit if you are going on a long ride, and tell someone your route.
- Check those areas that are in direct contact with tack to ensure that there are no lumps, swellings or sores, also that your tack is clean and smooth. Adjust it so that the horse is comfortable – straps not too tight, bit not too high, numnah not folded up under the panel.
- Mount from a mounting block, as this is better for your saddle, your own back and your horse's back.
- Do not allow your horse to move off until you ask him, as this can be dangerous. Remember to check your girth after 10 minutes, and during your ride.

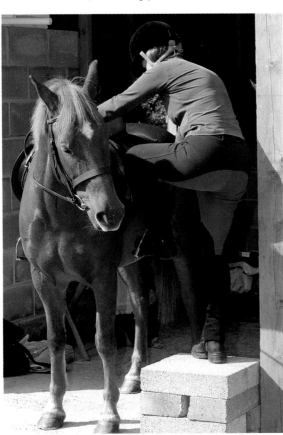

During work:

If the horse has been eating recently, walk for 20 to 30 minutes. Do not do fast or strenuous work (athletic trotting/canter/gallop/jumping) for at least an hour after eating.

- Do not ask more of your horse than he can do without distress. Learn to recognize when a horse is struggling – labouring, breathing heavily, sweating copiously – and if he is, stop and rest him with his head to the wind.
- Do not give sustained, hard work if the horse is not fit enough to cope with it; go home before he is tired.
- Learn to check his pulse from the saddle, inside the elbow.
- Go slowly over difficult terrain and let the horse pick his way on a long rein.
- If your horse loosens or loses a shoe, go straight home, or arrange transport.
- Always wear high-visibility clothing on public roads.

After strenuous work:

- Check tack areas, legs and feet for signs of injury, and treat accordingly.
- Try to return cool, but if the horse is hot, give him a few mouthfuls of water every ten minutes till his thirst is quenched, then water and hay/haylage ad lib.
- Give electrolytes if he has sweated a lot.
- Make him dry and comfortable, with or without rugs or bandages according to the weather, as soon as possible.
- Make sure he has a good bed or somewhere suitable to stale (urinate).
- Give a small, easily digested feed once he is cool, dry and settled – after about an hour.
- Temperature, pulse and respiration should be at resting rates after an hour. If not, or if the horse is showing signs of distress, including sweating and lack of appetite/thirst, call the vet.

HOLISTIC TIP

As well as stretching out the forelegs after girthing up before mounting, there are massage and shiatsu techniques you can use before and after work to help your horse's body cope with the work effort, and recover. [See pages 144 and 145].

15 The importance of daily health checks

Sometimes we are so busy that it is easy to overlook mundane tasks, or to miss noticing when a horse is perhaps off colour. If you make a habit of checking certain things daily, this can ensure that you spot developing problems, or that you do take action when something is clearly wrong.

Exactly what should I look for?

Make a habit of observing your horse's demeanour closely so that it becomes second nature to you to know when he is well or otherwise, when he is asking for something – and what – and when he genuinely does not feel like working, and so on. It should therefore become routine to you to check every day that:

- your horse has eaten and drunk his normal amounts;
- his bedding is not unduly disturbed, and that he has passed his usual amounts of droppings and urine;
- there are no unusual scrape marks on the walls, indicating that he may have been cast;
- there is no dried or fresh sweat on him, which could indicate that he had been struggling to get up for whatever reason, or has been, or is, in pain;
- his clothing is not unusually disarranged;
- he has no new injuries;
- he appears normal – calm but alert;
- there are no rat droppings in his stable, particularly near feed – rats can terrify horses, and they carry disease;
- you attend to messages from other owners if your horse is kept on a communal yard, whether these concern your horse or theirs.

The following checks should also be made frequently:
- Make sure paddock fencing and gates are secure and safe.
- Remove litter and dangerous items from paddocks.
- Make sure that the water supply is working.
- Take time to watch horses that are turned out together to check for bullying, and remove the culprits.
- Make sure that you always have enough feed and bedding in stock so that you never run out; order well in advance of running out.

- Every time you clean your tack check the stitching and its general condition; keep an eye on rugs and blankets, too, when these are in use.
- Make it a habit to constantly look for anything on which horses could hurt themselves; if there's something in their vicinity that could cause them an injury, they'll find it!
- Take your horse's TPR rates often, and always after hard work, or if you suspect a health problem. It is always useful to check the digital pulses (on the fetlocks) for developing laminitis: these will probably feel strong and 'bounding' if there's a problem.

16 Understand why horses need clothing

The right sort of clothing (rugs/blankets) can make a big difference to your horse's comfort, protection and, therefore, his health. However, it is important to learn when to use clothing, and when not to.

Do horses really need clothing?

Wild horses don't wear it, and there are plenty of domestic horses that don't wear clothing either, and many who are loaded up with far too much of it. However, getting the balance just right is the way to really help your horse.

Clothing horses is nothing new, and is a practice that has been going on since Man embraced the horse as a work animal, when he realized that clothing would increase its protection against the weather, and so help it make the very best use of its food.

Cold weather clothing

Working horses are clipped in order to reduce the amount that they would otherwise sweat, and so make it easier to clean and dry them after work. They therefore need

rugs/blankets to partially compensate for the loss of their protective winter coat. Also, when they are clipped, horses can feel very cold when they are left standing in the stable, because they cannot move about to keep warm.

Modern clothing can be either woollen or, more often, synthetic and usually 'breatheable' or permeable to allow moisture to be lost through the fabric. Horses sweat all the time, but it usually evaporates before we notice it.

Outdoor horses may not need clothing as long as they have their natural coats. The horse's worst enemies are wind and rain, particularly together, as these make him feel much colder than he would in still weather. Therefore, waterproof clothing is very helpful. It is also possible to buy 'horse chaps' to protect the legs from mud.

Hot-blooded breeds such as Thoroughbreds and Arabs can benefit from exercise clothing, sometimes waterproof, to cover the back and hindquarters, especially when they are older, and particularly if they are clipped.

Hot weather clothing

Insect attacks are the main problem in warm or hot weather, and they can make life torture for horses and ponies. Fly-proof, and particularly midge-proof mesh sheets are a great comfort to susceptible horses, and essential for those allergic to their bites.

A sheet may be used to protect the coats of show horses from bleaching in the sun. Some sheets also now protect against sunburn in pink-skinned horses. Also, lightweight summer sheets, preferably of linen, cotton or some cool fabric, can be used to protect the coats of stabled horses from dust and insects, although with the protection of fly repellents, they would probably be more comfortable without.

A NOTE OF WARNING

Never overload your horse with rugs and blankets. This is a very common mistake. Too many rugs make horses uncomfortable in the extreme, and causes undue pressure and weight on the body, excessive sweating, skin irritation, rubbing and mental distress.

17 Learn how your horse works

This may sound like a counsel of perfection, when in fact nobody in the world knows everything about how a horse works in mind and body. Most owners look to their veterinary surgeons for expert help and advice, and usually get it, but even vets are sometimes nonplussed. Fortunately it is not too difficult to acquire a useful working knowledge of the subject.

The important things to learn

Just as most people do not want or need to know how to service and repair their own cars, horse owners do not need to become vets in order to work their horses safely and to keep them happy and in good health. A moderate level of practical ability, backed up by some simple scientific knowledge of the whys and wherefores, is all that is needed.

- The first topic that you need to understand is the difference between a horse in good health, and functioning normally both mentally and physically, and one that is starting with, or actually has, a problem. A good knowledge of first aid is also essential.
- The next specialized topic of which you need a good understanding is feeding and nutrition. This is crucial, because 'we are what we eat and drink'. The horse feed industry is one of the most confusing to negotiate, but there is a way through the maze!
- Farriery and daily foot care are essential, because in the words of Mr Jorrocks, 'No foot, no 'oss.'
- Dental care is equally important.
- Maintaining a decent bed for your horse is a matter of common sense and hygiene. So many people would be horrified if their dog had a bed soaked with urine and contaminated with faeces, but think it's fine for their horse. It isn't. Learning to keep a decent bed is necessary.
- Understanding about fitness and gymnastic work to keep a horse athletically fit and supple is also important if he is expected to work, and this topic needs to be mastered to cope with the level at which you wish to ride.
- Grooming and turnout, believe it or not, are not essential, but it adds to the pleasure of riding if you know how to keep your horse decently clean, and how to turn him out for shows and events if you wish to compete. Grooming obviously helps to keep stabled horses clean and toned up, and helps you to spot skin problems. Even outdoor horses need basic brushing and inspection.

What can I do?

- First of all, ignore people who tell you that you can't learn anything from books – and I don't say this because I am a writer. From the dawn of civilization, writing in the form of clay tablets, scrolls and books – and now computers and the internet – has been crucial to learning.
- Read as many good books as you can, and try to make judgements, through observation, experience and recommendation, about the best ones. There are many excellent books being produced in the horse world today. Most books by people with 'paper' qualifications should be helpful, but there are many horsemen who are experts in their field (such as showing, jumping, event training and so on) who write informative books as well. Be prepared for the fact that experts will often disagree, keep reading and asking questions of reputable people, and you will gradually form your own ideas of what suits you and your horse.
- A riding teacher whom you trust and who appears to be kind and effective, not domineering, forceful or even cruel to your horse – and some are – is a real boon, particularly to the inexperienced.
- Surf the net by all means, although it is often difficult to make value judgements about what you read.
- Finally there are many courses, long and short, vocational and non-vocational, these days in the equestrian industry, from complete novice level to PhD. Distance-learning courses are useful for those unable to go away to college, and who live in areas where there are no local courses. Adopt a policy of lifelong learning – easy to do in the horse world, because horses always put you in your place and never fail to amaze you – and you will have a lifelong passion that will always be rewarding, and will become a reliable constant in your life.

Mind and body

The influence of environment on mind and body

A horse's environment is as important to his health and welfare as the way he is treated and managed. A good environment can undoubtedly influence his mental and physical health positively, whereas a bad one, or even a borderline one, can compromise these things or actually cause ill health, stress, insecurity and discontent.

It seems to be well accepted now that mental distress, however mild, actively favours the development of physical disease in humans and animals – but what constitutes mental distress? I think we can assume that the physical pangs of hunger, thirst, pain and discomfort will also cause a distressed mind, as undoubtedly will any feelings of fear or insecurity, frustration, boredom, loneliness, and general mistrust and unhappiness.

Many people ask how we can possibly tell if a horse is happy or unhappy, and sometimes even question whether or not horses experience happiness. I am always amazed when I hear this question, because to my mind there can be absolutely no doubt that horses and other animals experience happiness and contentment, as well as their opposites.

To know what makes horses happy we have only to look at how they have evolved, and at what kind of animals they are. Basically, they are herd animals that have evolved to live mainly on open grassland plains, exposed to predators – and if you think about it, this says it all. Thus in a good environment they have food (grass) always around, water and shelter within a reasonable journey, friends and relationships, and the feeling of safety provided by numbers and because they are totally free to escape, and to travel about finding supplies and resources.

Arguments continue about whether or not there is actually a herd leader, but there are undoubtedly matriarchal guides, and the males seem to act as possessive minders. The disadvantages of this kind of life and environment are the need to find shelter and water, and the necessity of living by your wits to recognize danger, plus the requirement for both physical speed and stamina to escape it.

In domestic life, all this translates quite easily and obviously, if rather basically, as the following:

- constantly available food (fibre) and water;
- having the liberty and space to run freely;
- congenial company;
- physical and mental security and comfort;
- trustworthy humans.

The first four requirements above should not be that difficult to provide, and this section should give you plenty of ideas as to how to do that in a domestic setting.

18 Understand your horse's natural needs

All mammals have basically the same mental and physical equipment, and the same needs, relevant to the individual. It should not, therefore, be difficult for us to work out what a horse needs in order to be mentally and physically healthy. Problems can arise when novice horse owners understandably take their cue from more experienced owners on their yard, assuming that they must know what they are doing – though sadly this is often not the case!

What do horses want out of life?

There is one overriding element that horses want all the time, and which covers everything else: they want to be comfortable, both physically and mentally. Physically they want to avoid anything that causes them pain, discomfort and even slight irritation, and mentally they want to feel secure – which they won't if they are physically uncomfortable or if they feel mentally distressed.

What can I do?

There are six basic elements that horses are probably aware of wanting most of the time on a daily basis, and which all come under the umbrella of comfort. These are:

1 Food: ensure that your horse has a constant supply of fibre – horses are 'trickle feeders'.
2 Water: ensure that your horse has a constant supply of clean water.
3 Shelter: ensure that your horse is not out for long periods without adequate shelter and/or appropriate clothing in extremes of weather.
4 Company: ensure that your horse's companions are friendly and do not cause him distress.
5 Space: horses need to feel that they have room to move around comfortably, and not have their personal space continually intruded upon by unwelcome visitors or unfriendly neighbours.

6 Movement: ensure adequate daily exercise – horses need to move around a good deal in order to keep healthy and satisfied.

Other aspects involved in comfort may only become obvious to horses occasionally, such as uncomfortable feet, badly fitting tack or a slipped rug; if they feel ill because of disease or worm infestation; if eating is painful because of sharp teeth; or if they feel the real pain of colic or laminitis. These issues involve owners also paying meticulous attention to veterinary, dentistry and farriery services, and to the horse's tack and clothing.

So take account of your horse's lifestyle, and the kind of animal he is, and care for him accordingly.

19 Make an outdoor space for your horse

Most equestrian premises have areas and corners here and there that are not put to best use. Converting them to what I call 'play-pens' to give stabled horses some relief from over-confinement is usually fairly easy and economical, and will make a great difference to the horses' wellbeing and occupation, both of which affect their health.

Why extra outdoor exercise and turnout areas?

Although modern stable management can offer many improvements in technical knowledge to do with nutrition, physiology and veterinary matters, it is clear that there are worrying and regressive tendencies developing as regards general management. The most obvious of these is the increasing trend towards keeping horses over-confined and under-exercised for long periods of the year – and sometimes they are kept like this permanently, an unkind and counterproductive practice, in my view.

Stabling horses for most of their day (sometimes all of it) is not a humane way to manage them, particularly if they are also on a limited exercise regime. Horses that do several hours' work a day, or are exercised for a major part of it, take to it better; for instance, many army and police horses live this way, as do the few working or commercial harness horses left living and working in towns or cities, that only have time out at grass occasionally.

It is noticeable that horses that are stabled nearly all the time often develop behavioural abnormalities beyond the officially recognized 'vices' or stereotypies; like the latter, these are almost certainly a reaction to frustration, distress and boredom, and they can, in turn, seriously affect physical health. Most privately owned horses and ponies that are made to live this way do so because many livery stables, unfortunately for the horses, now offer little or no turnout or grazing for much of the year; and if this is combined with only a short time at exercise, then it is no way to keep a horse or pony, in my view.

This situation can, however, be redressed, and the more reasonable and conscientious yard owners should be amenable to implementing the following suggestions, and owners who have their own premises will have little trouble in doing so. All it takes is a positive will and imagination, for the sake of the horses. Ideally, stables that open directly on to a small paddock, as in the photo on page 42, can make a pleasant facility for horses.

What can I do?

- The ideal is to have a space that is directly accessible from your horse's stable, so that he can go in and come out as he wishes. Old bull boxes, for instance, often had an adjoining pen so that the animal could be out if he wished, and a few studs have a similar facility for their stallions. Free will is as much appreciated by animals as it is by humans.
- If there is no room to the front of the stable, it may not be too difficult to make a second door leading to a space at the side of, or even behind it, which can be securely fenced off. It needn't be very big – even an area the size of the stable itself is better than nothing (ideally with something green, attractive and non-poisonous growing in it), although the larger it is, within reason, the better. If compatible neighbouring horses also have this facility they can socialize over the fence, and will be much happier than only being able to see each other, which is not enough.
- If a space adjoining the stable is not possible, have an imaginative look around your yard for any under-used or spare patches of ground that can be fenced off into small exercise and amusement areas or play-pens. An expensive gate is not essential: sliprails will do. The ground surface can simply be dirt, or have bedding laid on it if it is semi-hard. In larger spaces, however, horses may be inclined to buck and canter, so concrete, for instance, would not be safe.
- Play-pens can have a supply of water and hay or haylage, a selection of horse toys lying around, old rustic poles or logs for the horses to chew, old rubber feed containers, footballs, mineral licks or ground blocks, turnips, cabbages – anything safe they can play with and nibble at, if they wish. If they have access to a covered area they can be left out longer. Non-poisonous trees or bushes in the pen are welcome, in fact anything that will add interest and amusement for the horses.
- Research has shown that although this method may be a poor second to real grazing, it has a noticeable effect in creating calmness and contentment among otherwise imprisoned horses.

20 Establish a horse-friendly stable

If a horse is happy in his stable, he will regard it as a welcome haven from the outside world at times when that world is not kind. Thus good stabling provides protection from insects, blazing sun, pouring rain, uncomfortable wind, rock hard and rough land and deep mud.

The requirements of a modern stable

Many stables are only fit to keep equipment or feed in, and not a living animal, being poky, stuffy and dark, and no better than a dungeon. Today's requirements of a horse-friendly stable are as follows: it must

- offer shelter from extremes of weather;
- be cool in summer and fairly warm in winter;
- be strong enough to withstand kicking and shoving;
- have excellent ventilation without draughts;
- be large enough for the horse to be able to walk around in comfort;
- allow its occupant to touch and socialize with compatible neighbouring horses;
- offer food (fibre), water and dry, clean bedding on a slip-resistant floor;
- provide at least one outlook;
- and finally…be safe.

Clearly most stables do not meet these requirements, but many could be improved without too much trouble:

Shelter Ideally the stable should have its back to the prevailing wind, or if it is an American barn-type block, it should have one narrow end to it to minimize heat loss in winter and to allow for a cooling airflow through it in summer. There should be no gaps in the lower walls, as these could cause draughts.

Temperature and strength The walls and roof should be of good insulating materials to keep out extremes of heat and cold. Metal is useless, brick is good, hollow concrete blocks can be good, stone is wonderful for summer but may be very cold in winter, wood is very hot in summer even when lined, and most synthetic materials also need lining, although pre-fabricated, insulated panels can be good. Roofs in particular must be very well insulated to prevent extreme temperatures inside, and also condensation. Moreover they should be high enough to allow a horse to rear without hitting his head – not that he should want to.

Ventilation Ridge-roof ventilators are best, as warm, stale air always rises, and can then escape at the top. Other vents or outlooks |should be on walls other than the one with the door, so as to create a high cross-draught. Adjustable louvres are useful, as is Yorkshire boarding on the upper walls.

Size The latest research suggests that a stable 5m (17ft) square in size is needed in order for a horse to feel at ease and comfortable. Of course, most boxes are nowhere near this size, but all should allow the horse to sleep flat out, to roll, and to get down and get up in comfort.

Companionship The long-standing belief that horses should not be allowed to touch each other in stables is no longer considered correct by most behaviourists and behavioural therapists. Good management stipulates that friendly horses only

should be stabled next to each other, in any case. Also there should be a 'chat hatch' between boxes, or better, the intervening walls should be low enough to allow them to sniff each other and to enjoy mutual grooming.

Food/water/bedding A more or less constant supply of fibre (hay, haylage or short-chopped forage) and water should always be available, ideally in a ground-level tub, or in a corner box, or on the floor in a clean corner, as it is more natural for horses to eat at ground level, and their teeth and digestion operate more efficiently like this. Bedding should be truly clean and dry (not dusty, or contaminated with droppings and urine), and the floor should be slip-resistant (non-porous rubber or synthetic mats, sealed to the floor so urine cannot get underneath, are suitable).

Outlook In a barn, horses should be able to look into the barn and through an opening in an outside wall. In outdoor boxes, the front door forms one outlet and there should be another in a back or a side wall. This could be a flap of reinforced glass or synthetic material so that even if it has to be closed in extreme weather, the horse can still see out.

Safety In a stable there are any number of objects that are potentially harmful to the horse: watch for slippery floors, loose mats, protruding nails, poorly fixed fittings that could be dislodged by a bored horse, weak or damaged structures, exposed pipes or wiring, nails or blocks of wood in poor quality shavings bedding – in short, anything on which a horse could hurt himself.

21 Adapt stabling to benefit the horse's wellbeing

Many stables leave a lot to be desired as a welcoming home, but with a little imagination they can be greatly improved. The main problem in a livery yard – and livery horses must be the majority – is persuading the proprietor to let you make improvements, even at your own expense: so tact and diplomacy, plus a little persistence, are the order of the day!

Improving the ventilation

In practical terms, the simplest way to check whether or not the ventilation of a horse's stable is adequate is to be outdoors for some time, and then enter the stable and see if you can smell, feel or see any difference between the air inside and that outside. Ideally there should be no difference at all, apart from the fact that you should not be able to feel significant draughts. If you can see dust floating about, if it feels noticeably warmer than outside, or close or muggy or smells significantly of horses, then the ventilation is not good enough.

Mostly what is generally needed is a cross-draught as high up as possible, because you need to create air flow to change the air. Complicated fittings are not essential, although ridge-roof ventilators are ideal. Just try judiciously removing a few bricks or planks high up on an outside wall other than the one where the door is; you'll be surprised at the difference it makes.

If you have your own premises, there should be nothing to stop you installing kitchen-type extractor fans to suck stale air out of your stable/s, to be replaced by fresh air coming in through the door and windows. Fans are invaluable, and really come into their own on muggy summer days when there is no breeze and when horses brought in for the day away from sun

and flies simply stand in their stables and sweat miserably. But even in this situation, all that is needed is a good flow of air, and the fans create this. They are not difficult for a handyman to install, and are quite cheap. If you have a row of boxes, install one set on 'in' at one end of the row, and one set on 'out' at the other end. This works well for short rows of two or three boxes; otherwise, install fans on the walls diagonally opposite the doors in single boxes.

Providing a better outlook

Horses feel safer when they can see all around them. Stables with only one 'hole in the wall' can create a feeling of psychological pressure and maybe claustrophobia, and may not provide enough mental stimulation or interest. Try creating another opening on another wall (away from the prevailing wind) towards an interesting view. This opening could be like an upper stable door, but made of some safe, see-through material, so the horse will then still be able to see out even if you have to close it in bad weather.

Providing the best type of flooring

Many people opt for rubber matting these days. Having experienced several kinds, I find the best is non-porous rubber, fairly thick, and sealed to the floor. The porous kind is never dry because it absorbs the urine; with the type that is meant to allow drainage underneath, I find it really difficult to rinse out all the urine and dirt from underneath it; and with the completely non-slip sort, horses sometimes find the exposed parts difficult to walk and turn on, and my own mare badly twisted a fetlock. The best, in my experience, is slip-resistant material that is thick enough to be cushioning (therefore softer and warmer),

and so allowing you to use a little less bedding (certainly not none); non-porous for obvious reasons; and sealed to the floor to prevent movement, and to stop urine and dirt getting underneath. I find it well worth the investment.

Improving the insulation

If you insulate nothing else, insulate the roof to cut down on extremes of temperature and condensation. The roof or ceiling should be high enough for the horse not to be able to reach it so you can use something as simple as polystyrene sheets or tiles, although proper building-standard insulation would be better. Most local authorities have strict fire regulations, so check whether your proposed material meets their requirements; they should also be able to recommend suitable materials.

Converting a building

If you have a choice of buildings to convert to stabling, choose the strongest, roomiest, airiest, highest, lightest and driest building you can, with interesting outlooks. Indoor or outdoor pens, rather than stables, are often fine provided that the horse (depending on his type and constitution) can find shelter, security, company, food, water, interest, and decent underfoot conditions and/or bedding.

'THINK LIKE A HORSE'

Many former farm properties are now available to horses, and may have accommodation that is more attractive to horses than conventional stables. Be flexible, think laterally about what your horse needs, not what may be conventionally or traditionally offered, and try to think like a horse about his accommodation.

43

22 Keep your horse's stable dust free

One of the many problems with horses is that they have very sensitive lungs. They evolved to live outdoors, but most domestic horses spend at least part of their time – and some most of their time – stabled, breathing in very poor quality air. This prevents optimal lung function, and makes the horse prone to allergic conditions and diseases: he becomes what horsemen call 'stuffy' or 'thick in the wind'.

The presence of dust in the stable

Ordinary stable dust is largely organic, coming from bedding, forage, dead insects and the horse's body in the form of particles of skin and hair. It gathers on rafters, walls, the tops of kicking boards, window ledges and on the horse himself, and is easily disturbed by the slightest air movement. It floats around the air space and irritates the horse's respiratory system.

There are basically two ways that you can deal with the problem, as far as is practical:

1 Get rid of what dust there is.
2 Try to prevent as much dust as possible getting into the stable in the first place.

What can I do?

- To start as you mean to go on, first put the horse somewhere else

whilst you give the stable a good blitzing and get rid of all existing dust. Open all doors, windows and ventilation points, then remove all forage (hay/haylage/chopped fibre), and all existing bedding.

- Either get the stable professionally steam cleaned or power washed, or give all the rafters and ledges from top to bottom a thorough vacuuming yourself, removing all the dust, and also all the cobwebs which only harbour dust, and which actually do nothing whatsoever to reduce the fly problem.

- Wash down and disinfect the stable and floor with a horse-friendly disinfectant, and when dry, lay a completely fresh bed of material described as 'dust free', 'dust extracted', 'screened' or 'cleaned'. Ordinary straw and shavings do not qualify!

- Then put in your horse's forage supply, soaking any hay or dry haylage, and his water.

- Now you can return the horse.

CLEAN AIR RÉGIME

Make sure that there is an adequate airflow and cross-draught to help waft out what dust will appear. Use dust-free bedding and forage, always soaking hay and dry haylage. Grooming and mucking out both raise dust, so always muck out when the horse is out whenever possible and always with all ventilation points wide open. Do not maintain old banks in your stable (see page 126). Also, groom the horse outside whenever possible, tied with his head into the wind to blow the dust away from his nostrils.

23 Rug and clip according to the horse's needs

The golden rule for both clipping and rugging or blanketing is, don't overdo it. A great many horses are clipped when they don't need to be, or even shouldn't be; and just as many are so overloaded with clothing that their lives are made a veritable misery.

When is clipping needed, and what sort of clip?

The only horses that need clipping in winter are those who always sweat significantly during work. Clipping was originally a management solution for hunters that are often kept hanging around, wet with sweat, when hounds check, when they soon become seriously chilled. (Actually a traditional hunter clip, when the hair is removed from all but the saddle patch and legs, is really not suitable for hunters, who would be much more comfortable with a 'blanket' or 'chaser' clip that leaves the coat as a protective layer over at least their loins and hindquarters.)

If your horse does little or nothing during the week and is asked to do only light work at weekends (because he is not fit enough for anything else, since he does no work during the week), a bib clip could be useful. If he is a hot-blooded type he may not need clipping at all.

If you want to work him harder at weekends he will need exercising on at least two days during the week, in which case he could be given a trace, 'chaser or blanket clip. Horses in full, strenuous work could need a 'chaser or blanket clip, or even a hunter or a full clip if they have a naturally thick coat.

How to tell if a horse feels cold

Most unclipped horses with access to shelters and stables do not need rugs unless they feel the cold, such as old horses or 'hot-blooded' types. Most clipped horses will need some clothing, indoor or outdoor as appropriate, from a lightweight rug to a winter-weight

one, or a spring-/autumn-weight rug with a detachable liner. Exercise sheets are appreciated by sensitive horses in harsh weather.

To check if a horse is cold, feel the base of his ears, his belly,

flanks, loins and hindquarters with the flat of your hand, giving time for any warmth to pass through a natural coat. If he feels chilly, put a rug on him. Obviously, if he looks miserable, is hanging around the gate or shelter, is hunched up, trembling or shivering, he is cold. In fact dry weather does not usually cause a problem; it is when conditions are wet and windy, particularly combined, that will really cause a horse distress.

BEWARE OVER-RUGGING!

Stabled horses should not be over-rugged. Check whether they feel warm or chilly, and rug only as necessary. It is bad management practice to load a horse with rugs, even to the point that he sweats in many cases. This causes considerable discomfort, both physically as skin irritation, and also as mental distress, and it is altogether bad horsemastership.

45

24 Relieve boredom and avoid stress

In the feral state, horses are occupied nearly all the time. They normally have no physical restrictions on their movements, they have natural social interactions with their companions, and they eat on the move for roughly 16 out of the 24 hours. They sleep in snatches of about half an hour up to a total of around four to six hours, leaving very few hours for doing anything else. Filling their time with boredom-busting pursuits is therefore not an issue for them.

What toys can I use?

Giving a horse something to do with his stabled time when he is not resting or eating his hay is, to my mind, good and considerate horse management – provided, of course, that the toys are as safe as is reasonably possible. Horses are naturally curious animals, and although they like familiarity and routine, they do seem to like playing with toys.

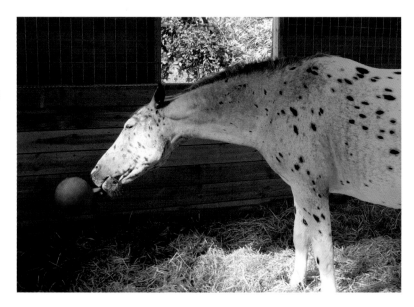

- Many years ago I knew an old horseman who used to provide his horses with toys. He would fill plastic lemonade bottles with water, and hang them to swing in a corner; he would give the horses footballs; provide a log for them to chew; or give them some harmless object to pick up and throw around. Most people thought he was mad. As a child I had no opinion – but I have never forgotten the sight of his stallion kicking his football against the walls of his stable and chasing it.
- Today, horse toys are regularly advertised in magazines. A favourite with many is the hollow ball with

small holes, through which nuts fall if the horse rolls it around the floor – not successful when bedding is down, so a bare patch has to be left. Another toy liked by many horses is a rope on to which are threaded licks of various flavours; and there are also various balls with handles, which some horses enjoy playing with.

- Tree branches (in leaf or otherwise) can be tied up in a bundle or stuffed into a hayrack for the horse to nibble

and play with; a sod of turf, soil and all, can be left in the manger; a turnip or cabbage might be welcome either tied up against a wall or left on the floor; or any of the toys mentioned earlier (the lemonade bottle, football and log) can all be tried to see which the horse likes.

- Like children, horses may become bored with one toy and will appreciate a change – and some aren't interested in toys at all!

25 Try a mirror in a stable

The traditional belief that horses must not be allowed to touch or sniff each other when stabled is still held firm in horse-world culture, even though behavioural research (and common sense) has shown it to be wrong. Horses crave compatible company, which much modern stabling design does not allow.

Using mirrors to prevent stress behaviour

Veterinary surgeon Dr Daniel Mills of the Department of Biological Sciences, University of Lincoln, England, has, over the past few years, done some valuable research on the use of mirrors in stables as a means of helping horses to feel less isolated and stressed and, therefore, less likely to feel the need to perform stereotypies (stable vices).

He and his team fitted mirrors in stables and found that they 'significantly reduced' the incidences of weaving and associated behaviours

such as head nodding and head throwing, and that horses appeared calmer and more settled. Photographs have appeared in the equestrian press of horses standing quietly by the mirrors placed in their stables.

Those interested in the interior design of houses will be well aware of how valuable mirrors are in making almost any space appear larger; they reflect light and an attractive view into a room when appropriately placed, thus giving a general feeling of space and light. There is no reason why this practice shouldn't also apply to stables, and if there is one animal that needs to experience a feeling of space and

freedom, even if they are only illusions, it is the horse.

The Equine Behaviour Forum has, in the past, featured articles by members on the reaction of horses to mirrors, and to their reflection in plate-glass shop windows. Even though horses cannot touch and smell their reflection, they do seem to regard it as another horse, and enjoy the company, in much the same way as caged birds do. Whether or not they realize that it is only their own reflection can probably never be decided.

What sort of mirror can I use?

Any mirror meant for use in a horse's stable must be as safe as possible and large enough to be effective, possible made of materials similar to, say, Perspex, and about a metre or yard square. Mirrors are sometimes advertised in the equestrian press but it could be well worth trying to find a few sources of synthetic mirrors via search engines on the internet. A friend of mine bought some mirrored squares from a DIY shop, but once they were installed she found that the fragmented picture they formed actually frightened her horse! When a full mirror was installed instead he immediately preferred it.

26 Supply companionship for a lone horse

We all know that horses are herd animals living in family groups, the only genetic outsider probably being the stallion; normally he would drive away the young colts as they matured, though sometimes he might allow subservient offspring to remain in the herd – but only if they were never a challenge to his role as sire (thus preventing in-breeding). Domestic horses are usually, unfortunately, denied the experience of living in a naturally structured herd, especially stallions, and some horses or ponies may not even have other equine company.

Providing company for lone equines

The first thing to do is to always try to ensure that a horse does have other friendly equine company. In small yards it may often happen that a horse is left alone, but in such a situation they usually come to realize that this is never for long, and that their companions always return.

There are cases where horses live alone for long periods and seem to adapt well, but this is unusual. Occasionally such horses may even attack other horses brought in as companions, or at least ignore them. Again, a few seem to be truly anti-social or unable to cope in a herd, not least those that were hand-reared as foals and never experienced horse manners and rules at a time when the brain could absorb such learning, when very young.

Most domestic stallions live lonely lives, and after puberty never get the chance to interact normally with other horses, male or female. However, this is not necessary in cases where they experience company from a young age, and it is continued as they mature. I well remember the Arab stallion, Scindian Magic, owned by Mrs N.D. Hardcastle of Norfolk, England, whose grazing companion was a pony mare called Glenda who taught him his manners and always grazed with him. I have known similar arrangements for other stallions. Small ponies have also been used in racing stables and studs as calming company for stallions and entire racehorses.

What can I do?

- If it is impossible to find another horse or pony as a companion for your horse, try a donkey. It's true that some donkeys and horses don't like each other, and some even share a mutual fear of each other – but often a donkey-horse friendship is quite good. Some people have sheep or goats as company, and yet other lone horses graze with cattle. Tales abound of famous horses that would barely be separated from their pet cats, birds, dogs and other animals.
- As a last resort, try to stable and graze the horse very near to other horses or animals so that he can at least, hopefully, be reassured by their presence.
- Some owners leave radios playing in the yard or barn as 'company' for stabled horses, alone or otherwise. In my experience this is always a mistake: if you study the horses you will see subtle, and not-so-subtle, signs of irritation and distress. And remember, like everything else in the horse's life, he has no control over his environment and is powerless either to turn the radio off, or kick it to bits, even if he wanted to.

27 At livery: put your horse's interests first!

How can problems at your livery yard cause problems for your horse? Simply because, if dissension has caused an unpleasant atmosphere, this can be picked up by the horses. If you are frustrated, unhappy or angry about anything, your horse will sense it, but may only show it in subtle ways.

Problems caused by people

There is no doubt that nearly all problems in livery situations are caused by people, and in my experience it is usually the yard proprietors who cause them, regrettably, either directly by not providing adequate facilities and services (or not allowing the use of them), or indirectly by refusing to intervene in problems caused by other horse owners and even staff. 'Yard politics' is one of the main reasons that so many owners move yards, and an uncooperative or incompetent yard proprietor is another.

In the UK, with the rise and rise of do-it-yourself livery, plus the demise of many of our riding schools due to the often untenable costs of insurance and business rates, riding and horse education is becoming harder to get for everyday riders who do not wish to take a college course (of which there are plenty). This is leading to those who are determined to ride buying their own, often quite unsuitable horses, and keeping them at DIY stables where there is no expert guidance.

Yard proprietors often do not want to become involved with the day-to-day activities of their yards, simply renting out boxes and grazing, and often very little of that. If arguments over turnout, supplies, theft of feed and equipment, anti-social or irresponsible behaviour and so on arise, and if there are problems of neglect or abuse of horses, owners are often left to sort it out amongst themselves. Moreover many yard proprietors have little knowledge of horses, very low standards themselves, or simply an uncaring attitude.

What can I do?

If you have that sort of proprietor plus trouble-making owners, there is little you can do but leave. If you only have one side of this problem to deal with, try to cultivate a diplomatic but firm attitude in dealing with them (although this is difficult when your blood is boiling, I know!) and enlist the help of similarly minded people (proprietor or owners) in solving the problems.

HOLISTIC TIP

In any livery situation, it is essential to keep a regularly updated list of *other* yards – private or commercial – where you could take your horse, even temporarily, if things became untenable at your current yard. Also, it may be possible to keep your horse mainly at home, renting grazing and the use of schooling facilities: it's an aspect worth investigating.

28 Make your field boundaries safe

Many injuries occur each year because horses hurt themselves on fencing. Most are unnecessary and only happen because unsafe fencing materials and construction were used. Another compelling reason for keeping horses well fenced in is that of 'strict liability' in insurance claims, whereby even if you are found to be not at fault, you are liable if your horse gets out of his field, or is let out, and causes damage or injury.

What constitutes high risk fencing?

The fencing of highest risk to horses is barbed wire. Horses are highly nervous creatures and may gallop around at high speed at the least excuse; in such a state of excitement some may try jumping the boundary fence, and ponies may try to push through. They will also often 'fence walk': they will trek up and down the fence line like a caged animal, particularly if there are other horses or greener grass on the other side. Barbed wire can cause horrific injury if a horse runs into it at speed or tries unsuccessfully to jump it.

Any kind of metal railing with sharp points anywhere – either intentional or unintentional – is also unsafe; so is ordinary sheep netting, because horses risk putting their feet through the mesh; and supports and stiles and concrete posts that protrude into the paddock, besides being unsightly, also constitute a health hazard in so far as they have the very definite potential to cause injury. Inherently weak materials such as chestnut palings, and insecure structures such as loose plain wire fencing and rotting wooden fencing should be cleared right away as soon as possible.

Gates and sliprails must be strong, and lockable at both ends. If they are weak and falling apart, and damaged so that the wood is splintered, and screws and nails are exposed, with insecure fastenings and holders and sagging posts – then horses will be able to push out, and intruders will be able to get in with no problem, and will have a free rein either to steal the horses or to let them out.

What constitutes safe, effective fencing?

- The best option is high, thick, prickly hedging, thick right down to the ground and at least the height of the horses' withers. Any other safe fencing of the same height is a good substitute. All posts should be sunk into the ground for at least a third of their length. Wooden posts and rails are traditional but expensive, taut plain wire is adequate, diamond or small rectangular wire mesh is good, and metal-reinforced flexible rail fencing is good.
- Electric tape fencing is useful for reinforcing poor or dangerous fencing, but not all equines respect it, and neither do intruders.
- Gates and sliprails should be very strong, as high as the fencing, and lockable at both ends. Gates should be filled in with mesh in at least their lower half. Try to have all field entrances opening on to private land, rather than public roads.

29 Build your horse a field shelter

Despite the importance of shelter to horses' comfort and contentment, most horse paddocks have little or none. Natural shelter is no protection from flies, rain drops off tree leaves on to horses' backs causing skin problems and discomfort, and leafless hedges offer little protection from winter winds.

Horses are outdoor creatures so why do they need shelter?

In natural conditions horses would live where their ancestors evolved, and would have the benefit of physical features that helped them to cope with the local climate. This is often not the case with domestic horses, many of which suffer greatly from exposure and extremes of weather. Feral horses, too, often live shortened lives, partly because of the rigours of outdoor life.

Any horse or pony will use a shelter when he feels the need, provided he is not afraid to enter it – and the usual reason for this is that another, bossy horse is keeping him out. If this sort of thing happens, the bossy horse should be removed.

What kind of shelter is best?

Any kind of protection that will shield horses from wind, rain, snow, sleet, insects and hot sun is better than nothing. Both side-on and overhead shelter are needed, and these are only effectively provided by a man-made shelter.

You can go the whole way and provide either a completely new building, or you can bear the cost of repairs to an existing building of brick, stone or blocks on a concrete base; alternatively you can use second-hand timber or even straw bales, with a simple roof on the driest part of the paddock. The main requirements are that it should have its back to the prevailing wind, be light enough to be welcoming yet provide shade,

and have an entrance high and wide enough not to put off horses from entering – say, a minimum of 1.2m (4ft) wide by 2.1m (7ft) high, although an open front is now commonly seen – yet remain dry underfoot inside. A size equivalent to 1½ stables is quite adequate for two animals.

PORTABLE SHELTERS

Portable shelters are available that do not normally need planning permission, although local councils vary in this. Their advantage is that they can be moved by a four-wheel-drive vehicle where needed, and faced north in summer and south in winter (prevailing wind permitting) for the northern hemisphere, and vice versa for the south.

30 Develop the best possible pasture

For most horses, grass is the cheapest, best and most natural food available. Horses evolved to live, breed, move athletically and thrive on just grass. In domestic conditions, grass is usually grossly undervalued, misunderstood and mistreated or neglected. Pasture should be far more than just a turnout area.

A suitable pasture for horses

Even if you have only a small space for your horse or horses, care of grassland can reap noticeable benefits. It is said that to provide significant year-round keep (food) for one horse you need about 1 hectare or 2 acres, with half as much again for each additional horse. As well as the food grown, the land provides important exercise space and freedom.

Horses do not need highly nutritious grassland, and indeed it can cause them considerable physical damage, particularly native ponies, cobs and the heavier type of horse and their crosses. Serious disorders such as laminitis, and various developmental and metabolic problems can be caused by the high sugar content of overly nutritious pasture. High nitrogen fertilizers, in particular, should be avoided; nevertheless grass does need feeding, and if necessary, advice should be sought from an equine-orientated company or, in the UK, the Equine Services Department of DEFRA (or your local Extension Agent in the US) as to a suitable fertilizer to use in spring and maybe autumn. (Possibly liquid seaweed or, if you can find it, organic farmyard manure, which also disguises the smell of horse droppings, would be best.)

Maintenance procedures

There are various maintenance tasks that should be addressed throughout the year in order to keep a pasture in good heart; these include:

- Land drainage (which does not need to cost the earth – unless you don't do it).
- Soil and herbage analysis.
- Rotovating and harrowing, fertilizing and topping (mowing).
- Reseeding and oversowing: suitable grasses for horse paddocks include ryegrasses, red fescue, rough-stalked meadow grass, smooth-stalked meadow grass and timothy, plus a low percentage (10 per cent) of wild white clover.
- Get rid of weeds: docks, nettles, thistles, broad-leaved plantain, chickweed, buttercup, and poisonous plants.
- Grow desirable herbs in a herb strip or patch: wild garlic, comfrey, burnet, chicory, yarrow, dandelion, narrow-leaved plantain and sheep's parsley.
- Avoid ploughing horse paddocks, unless they are in a really bad way, because this destroys the valuable root mat that reduces the jar to horses' legs when the ground is hard, and helps to prevent the surface from being cut up when they gallop about.

MAINTAINING PASTURELAND

Picking up horse droppings every two to three days during the growing season is very important to keep down internal parasites, as is applying selective weedkillers and fertilizers, as advised, when the land is resting. For continued productivity and wellbeing, each paddock in turn should rest for three continuous months every year. Land also needs harrowing and topping. after each grazing period.

31 Remove poisonous plants

Considering that horses have had millions of years in which to develop a fairly acute nutritional instinct, it is strange that they sometimes still fall victim to plant poisoning. Removing the plants means removing the risk to their health – but it is not always so simple …

Why do horses eat poisonous plants?

Most poisonous plants evidently taste nasty, so it is surprising that horses, normally choosy eaters, eat them. In fact the main problem occurs when the plants are dead and withered, when they seem to lose their bitter taste; very often they are eaten from the ground after a field has been topped or mown, or in hay, haylage or straw. Always take dead and dying plants right out of the field and burn them.

Very hungry animals, those bored with inadequate grazing, and those that do not normally have access to grazing and are desperate for anything green, may eat poisonous plants failing anything else; and a very few seem to acquire a taste for certain plants in the same way that people may acquire a taste for smoking or alcohol.

How can I get rid of poisonous plants?

You may have a problem if the land is not your own. A responsible landowner will take appropriate steps. Plants belong to different families, have varying methods of propagation, and are susceptible to different chemicals for killing them. A 'specific' product will kill specified plants, but not grasses; a general herbicide will kill everything, and you then have to start again.

In the UK ragwort (*Senecio* species) is a big problem, and the story has circulated for generations that it can be removed by digging it up or hand pulling. Most people's experience of this is that it makes matters worse, because one miniscule piece of root left in the ground will throw up new plants, and within a season or two your land will be smothered with it. Spraying with an appropriate product is the most effective way of killing poisonous plants, on advice from an agricultural or, preferably, equine consultant. It may put your land out of use for a while (so don't do all the land at once), but you may have no choice.

In the UK, the Equine Services Department of DEFRA (see your local phone book) can give you a comprehensive list of poisonous plants. In the US, contact your local County Extension Agent.

My livery yard will not take action: what can I do?

Apart from looking for another yard, make sure that your horse is not hungry when he goes out; then he should not be tempted to experiment with strange-tasting things, but hopefully will concentrate on eating grass or other forage provided in the paddock.

HOLISTIC TIP

For the odd few plants trying to get a hold, I find that if you cut them off at ground level and immediately put an eggcupful of salt on to the weeping stalk, they usually die.

32 Observe herd dynamics

One of the most popular topics with members of The Equine Behaviour Forum (see page 150) has always been that of 'kicking order' in herds. It holds an endless fascination, maybe because it seems to be easily observed, but maybe we've misunderstood what we're looking at because that's how our society is now structured. So what is really happening?

Is there a herd hierarchy or not?

Some scientists and behavioural therapists now feel that there is no actual herd boss and that horses depend more on friendships and mutually beneficial relationships than status unless they are overcrowded. An ears-back, nostrils-wrinkled scowl may express simply dislike rather than dominance. Horses who move away may simply not want a fisticuffs so are following their self-preservation instinct. Very sensible!

It usually seems to be a wise female (not always the oldest) who knows when and where it is best to graze, drink and shelter – but the other horses in the herd do not *have* to follow; they probably do so because equine society is herd structured, and such a structure offers safety, whether this is real or imagined.

Pair bonds...

Horses find separation from friends stressful for that very reason. Pair bonds can be frustrating and should be overcome by developing trust and respect between horse and owner. Humans must be quiet, firm and positive to impress horses! If you show yourself to have strong 'protector' qualities in order, and as long as you don't cause pain or fear – you're in.

...and bullies

Bully horses may be insecure due to lack of friends but can be dangerous to others. If your herd contains a bully, put him or her with a stronger, more self-confident horse or turn him out alone but in view of others. In livery yards, this situation can be problematic but yard owners surely have a duty of care, and they should make available alternative accommodation if necessary.

How can I tell where my horse fits in?

Observe who likes and dislikes him. Horses have an oval-shaped 'personal space' extending several feet around them into which only accepted others are permitted. Watch carefully and note who is allowed close to whom, whom your horse grazes shoulder to shoulder with, whom he moves away from and whom he himself shoos away.

This extends to stabling: it is bad management to stable enemies near each other, even with a friend on the other side, and can cause health problems due to stress.

33 Understand the male mentality

Basically, all that males are interested in is procreation: breeding and sex. This is in order to carry on the species and, in particular, their own genes -- although, of course, stallions probably won't consider the last two.

So where do stallions fit into the herd?

In feral life, stallions change according to who wins the latest fight for the job and the mares seem to accept newcomers without much argument. They just need a means of impregnation for nature's plan to continue, but stallion-less herds function just the same without them; there are just no foals till a new male joins the herd or grows up within it.

The core herd consists of a number of older mares who may be sisters or friends that have been together for many years. Many stallions expel male offspring from the herd when they reach puberty, whether they are his relatives or not. This ensures that only the stallion's own genes are passed on. They may expel their own female offspring as well when they reach puberty, which prevents inbreeding, but how stallions work all this out no one can really know. It's convenient to put it down to instinct. New stallions may also kill young foals sired by the previous stallion; this prevents his predecessor's genes from continuing.

The reason that stallions herd their mares and followers together is probably to prevent them being stolen by a rival stallion, not to protect them from harm. Normally they take no action if a herd member is attacked by a predator. Discretion is the better part of valour!

Stallions are not wholly without a sense of affection, however. They regularly mutual groom their mares and play with the youngsters, and behave just like any other herd member out of the breeding season. It is the mares, though, who decide when mating will take place, and all the stallion can do is wait and ask. When a mare is fully ready, she will stand for him.

And what about geldings?

It is estimated that about three-quarters of geldings retain stallion characteristics, particularly if they are cut late. If your gelding exhibits any of the above traits, including herding up mares and keeping away other geldings, mounting mares and trying to copulate, he's only doing what comes naturally – though to a lesser extent.

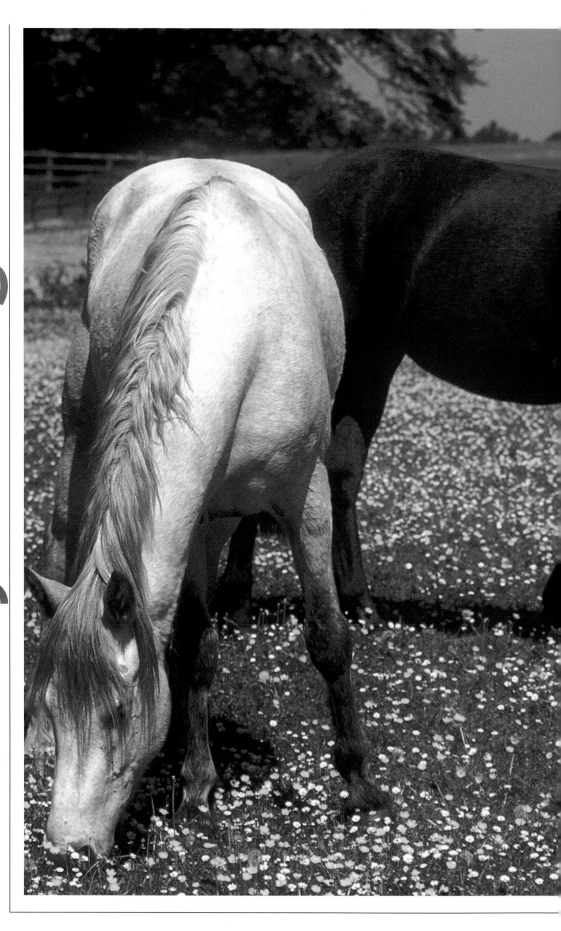

Healthy eating

Feeding for optimum health and fitness

Most horse and pony owners love feeding their horses. Feeding is extremely important, certainly, and placing a bucket full of tempting food in front of their horse gives great pleasure to most owners -- and most horses. The problems arise when owners feed what they want to feed, or what they feel the horse would like, rather than looking into what he really needs, or does not need. It is often hard to accept that, for instance, a particular horse really does not need cereals, and is actually better off without them.

Feeding has a great effect on health, both good and bad, and improving a horse's health can certainly be done by means of his feed, by not only feeding him what he likes, but in accordance with his requirements. The science of clinical nutrition (this means feeding as a means of healing, as opposed to simply nourishing) is also growing apace in the horse feed industry. There are now feeds for every type of horse or pony in every circumstance, and more and more feeds are appearing on the market aimed at specific health problems, laminitis being the most obvious example.

All the best feed companies now run free telephone helplines, and most also have web sites with information about their products, and about feeding horses and ponies in general.

The increase in the number of feeds and various additives available is not only the result of our knowing more about what horses need, due to scientific research in the field of nutrition, but also because horse feeds represent a viable commercial business. Bagged feeds and packaged supplements are popular with owners because they are easy to handle, and give them the feeling that they are buying the best for their horse. For the suppliers, they are relatively simple to present, market and transport, and it is not that difficult to create products for specific situations. Commercial feed companies do not get into the area of selling big-bale haylage, for instance, yet forage (fibre/roughage/bulk) is far more important for a horse than are cereal-based feeds. Selling it is just not so commercially attractive.

However, there is a great deal more to understanding feeding than simply buying the right-sounding feed from the shop or merchant, and I hope that this section will help you to make more informed choices about what your horse really needs, what he does not need, and what he should not really have.

34 Condition score your horse

It is easy, when you see your horse every day, to miss signs of him being over- or underweight. You get so used to his appearance that the fact that he is getting too fat or too thin just passes you by. Using a formal, objective method of assessing his condition or bodyweight helps you to keep him on track, and keeps your 'eye in' as to his true condition.

Why is correct bodyweight so important?

Athletic performance horses are known to work best at an optimum bodyweight. Expert and sensitive trainers know when their horse is just right and likely to give a top-rate performance, or when he needs to lose or gain a little bit of weight.

Even if your horse does not work particularly hard for his living, keeping him as near just right as you can will make him feel good; it will enable him to do more easily, and that bit better, whatever work you do want; and being the right weight is good for his health. Being either underweight or overweight is both stressful and counterproductive, but many owners cannot recognize this – or they simply refuse to do so.

As a guide to the optimum general bodyweight/condition of any type of horse, use the ribs as a criterion: you should be able to feel his ribs quite easily, without being able to actually see them unless he is turning away from you, when they may be just visible. This would equate to an overall condition score of 3, which is what you should aim at.

What can I do?

Part of your plan could be to condition score your horse each week, or at least every month, when you simply give him a score from 0 to 5 for his body condition or weight. The areas

you assess are the crest of the neck, the withers, behind the shoulders, either side of the spine, the ribs and flank, the croup and between the buttocks -- all visible areas where fat will either accumulate or be lost. The following explanation of condition scoring describes what you might expect to see in your horse for the values 0 to 5:

0 = emaciated

Poor ewe neck with narrow base, backbone easily visible and protruding. Ribs easily seen, croup and hipbones protruding; hollow flanks, no flesh between the buttocks.

1 = poor

Slightly better than 0.

2 = moderate to fair

Straight neck (no curved topline), narrow at base, but with a little tone. Ribs, backbone and hips easily felt as being bony, but not too visibly obvious; hollow under and around dock.

3 = good/correct

Neck showing some topline, firm muscle tone, spine can be felt, but not protruding, back well covered in muscle/flesh. Ribs not seen but easily felt, hips and hindquarters are covered, but 'hipbones' (wings of pelvis) can be felt; more flesh under tail.

4 = fat

Neck showing some crest and starting to become hardened, maybe with ridges of fat forming. Ribs cannot be

seen and are hard to feel, possible groove down the spine between pads of fat on the back; croup and hipbones hard to feel.

5 = obese

Hard, ridged crest, probably notable gutter down backbone, bulging shoulders and flanks. Ribs cannot be felt, 'appley' hindquarters.

How do I condition score, exactly?

- Get a notebook or clipboard and write down on the left the areas you are judging, with the date at the top of the column and space for the score underneath, so you can keep a running record over time. Make allowances for the horse's work or rest regime.
- Tie your horse up or get someone to hold him, and stand him up 'four square'. Stand a few yards or metres away from him, and imagine you've never seen him before. Get a good visual impression of him from both sides, from in front and from behind, of whether you think he's fat, or thin, or whatever.
- Now get up close and use your fingertips to really feel each assessment area – and be honest with yourself, for both your sakes. Resting horses may go up to a condition score of 3.5, and very fit ones down to 2.5, but there shouldn't be much more variation than that.

35 Work out your horse's ration

Most owners are familiar with the so-called 'golden rules' of feeding, but these are no real help when you have to make practical decisions. You need to observe your horse closely and change his diet according to his mental and physical response to what you have chosen.

What type of feed do I give, and how much?

1 Be quite clear as to what kind of equine you have. Is he or she:

- a Thoroughbred or Arab (hot blood), with fine physical features and maybe a temperament to match;
- a crossbred or 'warmblooded' type, with some hot blood and some so-called cold blood (most horses come into this category), a sort of 'half-way' type;
- a native-type pony or a cob, chunky, and of small to moderate height;
- a cold-blooded, heavy type, usually quite big, with coarser features and often a phlegmatic temperament.

2 Once you're clear on this (maybe with an expert, supporting opinion), condition score him.
The figures and amounts given below depend on a 'correct' score of 3. Fat horses will need a little less, and thin ones a little more.

3 Find out what his bodyweight is, because we feed according to weight, to be accurate.
Either take your horse to a weighbridge and weigh him without his saddle; alternatively, buy a weigh-tape, marked off in graded segments, from any tack store or feed merchant. Keep the tape flat and pass it round his girth area, keeping it vertical and pulling it just tight enough to press into his flesh -- and try to do this as he breathes out! Then read off his weight and write it on your condition-score record with the date.

4 Be honest about how much work he really does:

- Does he work hard, with a good deal of cantering, galloping and jumping – an eventer or a hunter? Or do strenuous gymnastic work – a dressage horse?
- Is he in medium work – riding club level, local shows and events, active hacking, half a day's hunting?
- Is he in light work or resting – the odd short hack round the block, or no work at all?

5 Consider the weather and his exposure to it.
If he is in cold conditions he will need more food than a sheltered, protected horse, or than he would if he were out but in mild or warm/hot weather.

6 Is he a good 'doer', or a poor one?
Does he seem to need a lot of food to keep weight on him (a poor doer, like some Thoroughbreds), or do you have a job keeping him slim (a good doer, like most natives and cobs)? Normally the more Thoroughbred blood that a horse has, the harder it will be to keep the weight on him; and the heavier he is, or the more cob or pony blood he has, the harder it will be to keep him slim -- though always consider each horse as an individual.

Choose the energy level

All reputable branded feeds give the energy level of the feed in megajoules (MJ) of digestible energy (DE) per kilogram on the bag. Generally, big bale, dry-ish haylage may have an energy content of about 8–12 MJ of DE per kilogram, with good meadow hay about 6–10 MJ of DE per kilogram. The energy level of good grass will be about 11–13 MJ of DE (not counting its water content) per kilogram.

- A heavy horse, cob, pony or good doer of any sort should have about 2 per cent of his bodyweight daily in total weight of feed, maybe a fraction less if he is fat or resting. Choose an energy level averaging 7–8.5 MJ of DE per kilogram.
- Other types resting or in light work should have 2.5 per cent. Energy as above.
- For medium work, give 2.5 per cent, but maybe use higher energy feeds (see next). Energy level, say, 8.5–10 MJ of DE per kilogram.
- For hard work, give 3 per cent of bodyweight and maybe higher energy feeds and/or added oil, which is energy rich. Energy, say, 10–13 MJ of DE per kg.

How much of what?

Research now indicates that probably only hard-working horses need cereals. Higher energy forages such as alfalfa can be used for medium work with the addition of soaked sugar-beet pulp and probably oil. Hard-working horses needing concentrates could have three-quarters of their ration as fibre/forages and one quarter as concentrates.

36 Recognize the health risk in over- or underfeeding

Does it really matter if the ration for your horse or pony is occasionally slightly under or over the recommended amounts? To be truthful, no it doesn't. But problems arise when owners do not spot changes in their horse's condition indicating that the ration is consistently incorrect, and fail to amend it.

The risks of over- or underfeeding

Put simply, if you overfeed your horse he will get fat, and as a consequence he may be put at risk of contracting equine rhabdomyolysis (azoturia), laminitis, heart disease or colic; he may suffer limb and joint strain through carrying too much weight, or be unable to work well or for long; or he may just become too energetic and excitable. You may also find that the saddle doesn't fit him so well any more, if it was bought for him when he was a reasonable shape.

If you underfeed him his energy levels will certainly suffer, he may contract digestive problems because of insufficient feed passing through his gut, he will become debilitated and short of nutrients in general, and this will adversely affect his whole bodily function, and not just his weight. As a result his immune system could be affected so he might fall victim to infectious diseases even if vaccinated, he may become anaemic and weak, and he will certainly not be able to work well.

What can I do?

Quite simply, condition score your horse every week, and keep a regular check on his actual weight. Feed him according to the advice given on pages 58 and 59, and if you are still not sure whether or not he is in fat, good or poor condition, seek the advice of a veterinary surgeon or nutritionist.

Many other owners, and ostensibly very experienced and knowledgeable owners and even teachers and trainers, may have wildly differing opinions as to what constitutes good condition in horses. Most people overfeed, particularly those involved in showing and dressage and those whose horses do little work, and this can affect their 'eye', making them unable to recognize correct condition. It is also true that many people like their horses 'well covered' (fat) because the rounded shape gives the impression that they are feeding their horses well. In this context, 'well' means too much, and perhaps so much as to put the horse's health at serious risk.

REMEMBER THE OLD ADAGE!

It has to be said that it is safer to very slightly underfeed a horse than to overfeed him. Keep a very close, daily eye on him, and remember the old adage: always reduce the feed before reducing the work, and increase the work before increasing the feed.

37 Feed holistically

Organic food is surely healthier for both ourselves and our animals, but holism also involves techniques of feeding. Although we are becoming more aware of these things, total holism is a counsel of perfection for most of us – but at least we can try to get as close to it as is practicable.

What does feeding holistically mean?

Feeding holistically means feeding as naturally as possible, having regard to the wide-ranging effect that food has on the body and mind. Horses evolved as grass eaters with unlimited freedom, so they should be allowed to graze as much as possible and on large areas of poor to moderate pasture. This is an impossible dream for most owners, and is where many have to compromise.

What can I do?

- Pressurize livery yard proprietors for more grazing and decent turnout, with forage, all year round. Make this your first pointer when ringing potential new yards: if all owners firmly insisted on this, then things would eventually improve.
- Pester feed companies for organically produced feeds and supplements. This means crops (grasses, sugar-beet pulp, carrots and cereals) produced without artificial fertilizers, pesticides, weedkillers and preservatives, produced to the standards of the Soil Association. Feeds of Conservation Grade, not quite so stringently produced, are a very good second. Any vitamins and minerals added should be organic and natural, not synthetic. Customer power is considerable, so use your phone and start nagging.
- Make the basis of your horse's diet forage (fibre) – hay, haylage and grass. Today we have several, indeed many, good brands of forage, both long and short-chopped, of different energy grades suitable for any horse or pony in any job: this includes hay and haylage and bagged, short-chopped forages.
- If a nutritionist has advised that your horse needs cereals, scatter them in the top few inches or centimetres of a large tub of short-chopped forage so that they fall down through it and he gets a slow intake over many hours as he munches through his fibre. Horses don't naturally eat separate meals.
- Feed from ground level. This enables correct jaw action,

tooth wear and mastication, and improved mental and physical comfort and digestion.
- Experts in holism are telling us not to use rubber or plastic containers for feed and water as they can leak chemicals to which some animals are sensitive, causing digestive and metabolic problems. Old ceramic sinks and pots and stainless steel are said to be safest.
- If you use supplements, try to use organically produced herbal ones. Quiz firms selling herbal products about their sourcing and production processes, and don't accept hazy, evasive answers.

38 When to use vitamin and mineral supplements

The field of vitamin and mineral supplements is one of the most confusing for horse owners to cope with, because the choice is so wide and varied. Why are there all these products? Are they really needed? If so, which does your particular horse need? And how do you choose?

Your questions answered

Supplements are relatively cheap and easy to make, they are easy to package and transport, and they have a mystique about them that makes them easy to sell. That's why there are so many. They are not magic spells, but they might be needed in certain circumstances (see below) according to your horse's diet and situation. You should choose after taking professional advice.

So how should I use supplements?

Supplements come in two main types:

- Broad-spectrum or general, containing a wide range of vitamins and minerals aimed at bringing a poorly balanced or poor quality diet up to standard, or used to top up a diet containing few or no cereals.
- Specific, containing one or a few balanced substances aimed at correcting deficiencies, creating a balance, or to help with particular problems such as poor growth and development in the young, replacement of electrolytes or to help with poor horn quality.

Most reputable feeds will have 'vits and mins' added in a balanced form, but if your horse needs less than recommended, you may need a broad-spectrum supplement in a lower dose. A specific supplement should only be fed on the advice of a vet or nutritionist.

Supplements can be synthetic (most are) or natural (such as herbal ones). Holistic professionals always recommend natural ones where possible. They may be dried herbage, pellets, powders, granules or liquids. They all need storing in cool, dark conditions in clean, closed packs to keep well; be aware that they could start to lose their properties after the 'use by' date on the pack.

Remember: They must be used strictly in the amounts recommended by your adviser or the maker. More is not necessarily better, and could cause health problems.

WHAT ARE VITAMINS AND MINERALS?

Vitamins are organic substances needed in very small amounts for normal metabolism (the processes of life) to take place. Deficiencies can cause various diseases, but so can imbalances (incorrect proportions) and overdoses, although the body can cope with many of these, and can also make some vitamins in the body.

Minerals are inorganic substances needed in varying amounts. The major minerals are needed in larger quantities, but the trace minerals or trace elements are needed in minute amounts. Electrolytes are electrically charged types of mineral. Again, mineral deficiencies, imbalances and overdoses can cause problems.

39 Consider balancers for the horse under stress

In recent years, yet another new feeding product has come on the scene: the feed balancer. Is this just another ruse to get us to spend our money? What are balancers? What are they for? And does my horse really need one?

The difference between a balancer and a supplement

We are all familiar with 'compound' feeds – that is, feeds made up of several ingredients blended together, such as in cubes and coarse mixes. Balancers come mid-way between such feeds and vitamin and mineral supplements. They do contain vitamins and minerals, but also protein, carbohydrate and oils. They are normally conveniently produced as small pellets, and may be fed in amounts somewhere between those of feeds and supplements. Thus in effect, balancers are highly concentrated compounds.

Does my horse need a balancer?

Not if he is in normal health and body condition, and is not particularly stressed: if he is under stress this could be because he is old, or run down, not growing or developing well, recuperating after illness, in hard work, a poor doer, or the hypertense sort who worries weight off – and so on.

If your horse does not appear to be achieving optimum health and condition on his normal, sensible regime, a balancer could well help him. It can be added to any type of feed with the aim of adding condition without either over-taxing the horse's appetite or making him hyperactive or explosive.

The balancers currently available (and there will doubtless be different sorts in the future) are normally quite high in protein, and this sort of boost is often what is needed by the types of horse or pony under stress, as described above. Protein is needed to make body tissue in all categories of horse or pony, and some may need more than is found in most feeds.

As with any specialized, concentrated feed product, it is essential to refrain from feeding any that your horse doesn't need, or that isn't suitable. Take expert advice from your vet, or from a nutritionist at the firm whose feeds you use – or, of course, from an independent nutritionist – to see if a balancer really would help. Follow the directions on the pack, and monitor your horse's progress carefully.

40 Feed from the ground to optimize food conversion

Eating from the ground is one of those things that horses do best, and this kind of 'doing what comes naturally' takes up most of their time if they are given that chance. It has been noted that horses fed fibre from ground level in their stable spend longer contentedly munching than those fed from higher levels.

Why is ground level best?

The horse has a long head on the end of a long neck that contains the oesophagus, gullet or 'food pipe' down, or rather up, which his food passes to the stomach. It is pushed up by the same wave-like, squeezing movement called peristalsis that operates in the intestine. When the head and neck are stretched out downwards they are in almost a straight line, so there is no kink in the throat to create an obstruction, however slight, to the passage of food, and so there should be no discomfort in swallowing, and no discouragement to spend time eating. We are all probably tired of hearing that feral horses spend roughly 14 to 18 hours a day grazing, but it's true. Even when given ad lib forage, stabled horses do not eat for this long, so anything that encourages a stabled horse, or one on non-grass turnout, to spend more time eating, is good.

Furthermore the jaws work in a slightly different way when the head is down (this is discussed later), which makes the formation of hooks on the cheek teeth less likely. The food is chewed and mixed with saliva better, so making for better preparation and digestion. Finally the head-down position is beneficial to a horse's physique and topline, stretching the tissues along the back and causing a certain amount of belly lift – just what we want.

What can I do?

- Make sure that mangers are fixed with their top no higher than the horse's elbows, and preferably use ground mangers: this will mean he is eating with his poll below his withers at least. Most owners, anyway, feed from buckets or bowls on the ground.
- Do not feed long fibre from high haynets, otherwise horses will spend many hours developing all the wrong muscles in the neck, eating at an unnatural, uncomfortable angle, with a poor chewing action and a lost opportunity to stretch the topline.
- Feed hay or haylage on a bare piece of floor, or in large tubs in a corner. For horses that pull long forage around the floor, there are large hay containers designed to be fixed at ground level, from which the horse can pull only a mouthful at a time.
- Short-chopped forages can also be fed in large containers on the floor, fixed to the wall if necessary, so you can provide your horse with an alternative source and taste, as well as his normal long forage.

41 Soak hay to avoid respiratory problems

Soaking hay is generally regarded as a nuisance and another chore, as if we didn't have enough to do, anyway. Rumours abound as to the best soaking technique, and even some experts disagree. So do we really have to soak hay, and what is the best and most practical way to do it?

My hay isn't dusty: why should I soak it?

Horses' natural feed, grass, is normally moist to wet, although there are times when it is drier. Grass has a fairly high water content, and young grass in particular, and this is what horses are suited to eating: basically they like damp and moist food.

Dried grass (hay) can develop fungal spores if it is stored in badly ventilated conditions and heats up too much. Some bacterial contamination can also become established whilst the cut fodder is in the field – even apparently superb hay will have some dust, although we cannot see it. Furthermore levels of contaminants do not have to be high to trigger allergic respiratory disease, which may be slight or more problematic in susceptible horses.

What can I do?

- For one horse, probably the most practical way to soak hay is to put a full haynet into a clean tub and fill it with cold water. Soak it for about five minutes, till it has stopped bubbling, then hoist it out and hang it up to drip. When it has stopped dripping, give it to your horse either in the net (tied no higher than his head), or tipped out into his tub. The bottom of his tub will need to be quickly cleaned out every day.

- Soaking hay for long periods leaches out nutrients, reducing the feed value of the hay and giving the water the chemical properties of raw sewage, it is said. Soaking for only five minutes, though, swells the particles and spores to too large a size to be inhaled into the horse's airspaces (which is the whole point of soaking) and retains most of the nutrients. If the hay dries out, however, they will shrink again.

- The water should be changed after every soaking. If you only soak for this short time, you can safely pour it down a drain or into a watercourse. You should not do this, however, if you soak for a longer period because it

becomes equivalent to a pollutant. There is no need to soak for a long time, in any case.

- For yards with several horses, special tipper troughs are available that will take two small hay bales at a time. Cut the twine to loosen the bales, fill the trough, soak the hay until the water stops bubbling, then tilt the inner container so that the hay drips into the trough, which can later be emptied.

42 Feed the natural way: more forage, fewer concentrates

Most owners seem very anxious to buy sacks of feed, normally cereal-(grain-) based, to give their horse or pony. A culture has grown up that regards starch-rich concentrates (cereals) as essential, and implies that you are not feeding your horse 'properly' if you do not give him 'proper' food. However, the picture many of us have of wild or feral horses galloping over grassy plains, free as the wind, should tell us as plain as day what is the horse's natural food and the food he has evolved to cope with best: it is grass.

Why should forage predominate in a horse's diet?

There are no truly wild horses or ponies left in the world: they are all technically classed as 'feral' because at some point in their lives or ancestry man has interfered with their lifestyle and breeding.

Horses and all their more recent ancestral types have been grass eaters for many millions of years – not just herbivores eating other plant material as well, but specifically grass. They evolved to trickle feed (eat almost continuously) on grass. In the late summer and autumn of the year they would eat grass seeds as well as the rest of the plant, which helped to build them up for the long, hard winter to come. Mankind then took these early grass plants and seeds and started to 'manage' them, and gradually bred them into the greatly enhanced and nutritionally concentrated cereal crops that we in the western hemisphere now know as wheat, oats, barley and rye plus maize.

So horses did eat grains, but they were puny compared with today's plump, starch-rich cereal grains: and there, in that little word 'starch', lies the problem. The horse's evolved digestive system has a capacious lower end where the most serious business of the day and night takes place – the large intestine, where grass and its modifications hay, haylage and straw are digested by microscopic creatures to produce horse-friendly fuel, mainly cellulose-based, which gives the horse ideal slow-release energy.

Starchy cereal-based energy is a different matter. It is digested higher up the digestive tract in the small intestine (the emphasis being on the word 'small' because it isn't so necessary to horses, being grass digesters and not so much starch digesters).

Food is prepared in the mouth by being chomped up and mixed with alkaline saliva. Fibre takes twice as much chewing as concentrates, so absorbs more saliva. When starchy grains (and feeds made from them) are in the stomach, they therefore take with them less alkaline saliva to counteract the acid gastric juices in the stomach. Another problem is that acid is produced in the stomach continually whether or not there is food present, but saliva is only produced when the horse is eating. This creates a general shortage of alkali in horses on high concentrate/low fibre diets, and is felt to be why probably many of them have stomach ulcers.

If starch is fed in fairly large quantities to give a horse energy for work (and few horses really work these days) or because he is hard to keep the weight on, and so on, any excess starch not able to be digested on its way through the small intestine spills over into the large intestine, which is not best equipped to deal with it. Poor digestion can result in the formation of toxins that can cause behavioural and physical problems (horses may, in particular, become 'fizzy' and develop itchy skin and poor coats).

What can I do?

- If your horse does light to medium work, feed him mainly or entirely on fibre – hay, haylage and grass.
- There are high energy forages now (long or short-chopped) made from alfalfa/lucerne, grasses, and some straw (usually oat or barley), and some contain other energy-giving nutrients such as oils, which can cater for the needs of most amateur owners' horses.
- As a horse's energy needs rise, feed the highest-energy fibre you can find, and top up with soaked sugar-beet pulp, oil and maybe a competition mix containing other high-energy foods, with as few cereals as is practicable.
- If you do feed cereals, feed them in as small quantities as possible to achieve your aims, and spread them over as many feeds per 24 hours as you can.

43 Resist the power of advertising

Every horse magazine you pick up these days has much of its space taken up by advertising, and a lot of that is feed advertising. It can be really confusing reading all the adverts, and the language used can be very persuasive. If your mind is spinning at the end of it all, that's not surprising. How do you sort out what your horse really needs?

Assess the advertisements

When you read an advert, try to read between the lines and decide what it is really saying, what it doesn't say, and what kind of horse this product is really aimed at. The product may be excellent of its type, it may be ideal for your horse – or it may be the last feed in the world that he in fact needs.

If you see an advert that claims the product will put topline on your horse and pictures a show or maybe dressage horse, this will mean condition – weight – and it won't be what a good doer or an overweight horse needs. If you see one that says it will optimize your horse's energy output and there is a picture of a horse sweating, jumping or galloping, it is clearly aimed at hard-working performance horses, and will not be what a horse in light work, or no work at all, needs. A third example may say that this feed enables your horse to eat like a horse, or it will help to guard against stable vices, or is non-heating – a feed that is good for his digestion. Or it will use some other term indicating that it will not go to your horse's head, that it is aimed at horses in light to moderate work who can't take or don't need cereals: in other words, it will be high in fibre.

Assess your horse

We have already said a good deal in this book about different equine types, workloads and lifestyles. Re-read those sections and be honest with yourself about your horse's type (is he a good or a poor doer, a Thoroughbred, cob or pony) and how much work he really does (virtually none, light, moderate or hard).

Then, if you like, ring the free helpline at the company whose feeds you use or are interested in, or whose adverts you find appealing, and ask their advice. Not only is it against their long-term interests to give you poor advice, but also they will surely have a range of feeds and can advise you on the one best suited to your horse.

44 Alter feeding to manage difficult behaviour

There are various reasons why a horse may be over-energetic, scatty, fizzy, or show difficult behaviour under saddle, such as serious shying, bucking, rearing, plunging and so on. Most people blame the feed without taking obvious steps to change it; but there are other reasons.

Why is my horse like this?

It is perfectly understandable to be nervous about riding a difficult horse or pony. It is not clever to ride a horse that feels too much for you: it is foolish, pointless, and possibly dangerous. Ignore the taunts that may come your way, and get to the bottom of the matter.

You must consider that he may be in pain from his tack, including his bit or rugs; he may have toothache, an injury old or new, or poor eyesight, a mare may become difficult every time she comes in season, or bad behaviour may be associated with a bad memory in a certain situation, and so on. Get your vet to give the horse a thorough check, and discuss these things.

You will never change a horse's temperament, and bad memories can be hard to overcome, but most horses can be greatly improved with a low-energy diet, grass turnout, plenty of long, steady but sufficiently taxing exercise, and calm, firm, positive handling and riding.

What can I do?

- Put your horse on as low an energy diet as possible, but plenty of it to keep him occupied. Reduce the time he has on high-energy grazing in the

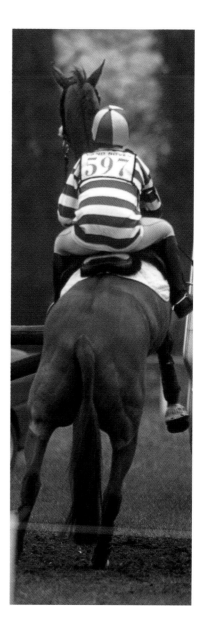

spring; otherwise grass can be ideal, because it is a complete feed that has a calming effect on horses.

- When stabled, give him a tub or a manger full of different low-energy, short-chopped forages (about 7.5MJ of DE per kilogram), plus nets of hay or maybe haylage mixed with oat straw if you can get it.

- Do not give him feeds with cereals in them, even if they claim to be 'non-heating'. If you want to give him a bucket feed because he expects one, make it damped short-chopped forage with sliced carrots or apples. This is also a good vehicle for a broad-spectrum vitamin and mineral supplement that he may need on such a diet, and for possibly giving him a herbal calmer, which may well help.

- Have lessons from an experienced, empathetic teacher to help you cope with his high jinks – but do not stand for the horse being tied down or beaten up (though a standing martingale may help to prevent you being knocked in the face).

- If the horse is still wild and difficult on this sort of regime, he either has some other problem (clinical or behavioural), or he just has that kind of temperament – so you will need to think hard about your future together, and you will have to make an appropriate decision.

45 Store feed wisely to prevent it becoming a health risk

Horse feed is expensive; it also spoils easily, and its value and nutritional content can easily be ruined by bad storage. Feeds are almost entirely organic in origin (that is, they are made of ingredients that were once alive), and when dead, they begin to rot unless they are preserved in some way. Good storage can optimize your feed's usable life.

What are the main things to consider when storing feed?

All feed concentrates, supplements, balancers and root feeds (sugar beet, carrots) need cool, dry, dark conditions. Carrots and other roots require ventilation or they become 'sweaty' and go bad more quickly. Hay and haylage need dry conditions, ideally out of direct sunlight.

Fibre feeds packed in plastic sacks normally have ventilation holes in them (unless vacuum packed), which, of course, let moisture in as well as out. Therefore, just because something is packed in plastic it does not mean that it can be left in the open. So it is important to check the bag.

What can I do?

- It should be possible to leave plastic-wrapped haylage outside in all weathers, but check that the plastic has not been pierced by machinery, animals, birds or anything else: air getting in will allow the deterioration of the crop, which could make the forage unsafe to feed.
- Bales of hay, on the other hand, are traditionally stored in open-sided

barns where exposure to rain can ruin them. Nutrients are leached out, and the outsides of such bales are worthless. The main point in hay storage is to keep it well ventilated, but protected from rain, with generous spaces between groups of bales.

- Feed rooms must be cool and airy, and any spills must be swept up at once so as not to encourage rats.
- The ideal feed containers are still large galvanized bins, although many people use plastic dustbins. Exposed sacks can be torn by rats, which can contaminate your feed

and infest your entire premises – remember that they can become very brazen and they carry diseases that are transmissible to humans and animals. Rats on the premises invade stables at night and can really frighten horses.

- For rat control, keep cats and terriers, and keep your whole place clean and free from spilled feed.
- Feeds containing sweeteners (including molasses), and some supplements would be best kept in a large refrigerator set on low in summer. This is also useful for storing phenylbutazone (and some other medicines, and first-aid products in hot weather). 'Bute loses its bitter taste when it is cold, and so may be easier to administer to some animals if used from the fridge.

SCRUBBED AND CLEAN

Never tip new feed on top of old feed. Put the new stuff in a different bin, then clean out the old one; when empty, it will be ready for the next delivery. Do not leave traces of cleaning material inside it, as this will taint the new feed. Rinse and allow to dry very thoroughly.

46 Understand feeds and feed labels

We all know how tricky it can be to choose the right feed for our horse. Puzzling over the analysis panel or feed label that gives the amounts of the ingredients contained may not be much help if you have no scientific, and specifically equine scientific, knowledge. You are not alone!

Where do I start?

The name and type of any one feed should tell you whether or not it will suit your horse: for instance, if you only hack around at weekends, you don't need a competition mix. Look firstly for the energy content (as explained earlier, see p. 59) to see if it is right for your horse. If this is not given, ask the merchant to ring the maker, or ring them yourself, because you do need to know this.

It is said, with some justification, that if the energy level is right for your horse the protein level will be, too – nutritionists know their job! Horses don't need as much protein as was formerly believed. Those fed for maintenance (resting and 'ticking over') are fine with 8 or 9 per cent protein, those in light work with 10 or 11 per cent protein, medium work about 11 to 13 per cent protein, and hard work up to 14 per cent protein. Feeds for debilitated, convalescent and breeding stock should be about 14 to 16 per cent protein. Check these against the type of feed and energy level you are considering, and you should find that they probably agree with the above.

You should look out for the following information on the bag:

- The oil content should also correlate with the energy and protein levels. For light work, 2–3 per cent oil may be included, with up to 10 per cent for strenuous work at the other end of the scale.
- The levels of vitamins and minerals (the latter expressed as 'total Ash') will also be correct if you are buying a branded feed from a reputable firm. There should be a broad spectrum of these included, and you really do not need to worry about the analysis.
- There will be a 'best before' date on the panel, after which vitamins are not guaranteed to be 'present', at least, not in the levels given on the analysis panel. Be sure, therefore, not to buy feed that you cannot use up before that date.

- Finally, check the ingredients section, because if you don't want cereals, you need to be sure that there are none. Just because something is described as 'cool' or 'non-heating', it does not mean that it is cereal free, and animals that are sensitive to cereals can still react badly to such feeds. You should therefore look for wheat, oats, barley and maize/corn.
- It is as well to keep your analysis panels for a while so that if the feed causes any problems the company can trace its production from the various numbers on it.

47 Know when to feed, and when not to feed

We all know that horses are designed to eat almost constantly, and normally it is best for them to do so: eating and running are what they're all about. However, there are times when a horse should not eat, or must not eat, because it could compromise his health, or exacerbate an existing health problem such as colic.

Won't depriving my horse of food be bad for his health?

Under normal daily circumstances, yes it certainly could. The horse's digestive system works best when there is always some food passing through it for most of the 24 hours. This system is particularly important for the health of the essential micro-organisms in the large intestine, which start to die off if they do not receive food for even a very few hours.

So when should a horse not be given food?

- Don't feed within an hour of hard work, and two hours if the work will be fast and strenuous – but do allow water, which is essential to help avoid dehydration. If horses work hard soon after eating, blood will be diverted from digestion to muscle function, so digestion will be poor, possibly resulting in colic. Also, the expanding lungs can press on the stomach, interfering with its action, and vice versa.
- In suspected colic cases, remove all food, and bed the horse on shavings, as further intake of food could make the situation much worse.
- Do not feed whilst the horse is still hot and blowing after hard work because, again, the blood is being directed to the muscles to help them recover. Wait till his temperature,

pulse and respiration rates are back to warm-up levels, then give some grass or hay; give a small feed when he is cool and dry, but not before. Do give a few mouthfuls of water every ten minutes or so, however, till the horse is cool, and then give unrestricted access.
- Never be tempted to feed if your vet has told you not to do so: you could

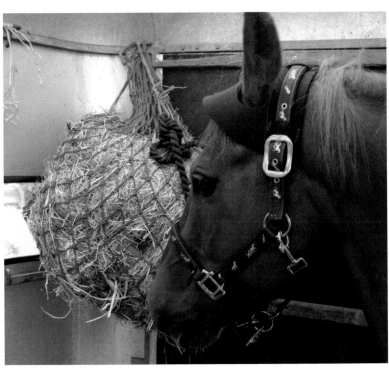

endanger your horse's life. Always obtain full feeding instructions at every vet visit in cases of ill health.
- If your horse has had an accident or experienced trauma, and particularly if he is in shock, his digestive system will not be geared up for

eating. Tension, as in humans, can cause indigestion, and in horses, colic. Wait till he is calmer (probably with veterinary intervention), then possibly graze him in hand or give hay before restoring normal feeding.
- In laminitis cases, give only hay and water and seek veterinary advice.
- Remember that travelling can be very stressful, and the horse can

be using unaccustomed muscles to keep his balance; an hour in transport can be equal to an hour's work. Hay or haylage during the trip is one thing, but a concentrate feed just before, during, or immediately after a journey is a bad idea.

48 Recognize the relationship between feeding and 'vices'

It's true that no one has ever yet cured a confirmed crib-biter or wind-sucker: that's the bad news. The good news is that these, and other so-called 'vices', can often be greatly lessened by remedial, correct feeding. Poor feeding can trigger them off, while intelligent, practical, corrective steps can greatly lessen their occurrence.

How feeding can influence stereotypies

What were for generations called 'stable vices', and regarded as 'evil' or 'wrong' behaviour by horses, are now called 'stereotypies' and recognized for what they are: non-productive and repetitive actions sometimes shown by animals (and people) in insoluble situations such as imprisonment. As far as horses are concerned, it is considered that these actions are employed to help them cope with the distress of an unnatural environment and lifestyle. Placing a horse in such a situation, which is extremely common, is very bad horse management.

It is known from scientific research and studies that giving a horse ample year-round pasture turnout (not a mud patch or a dust bowl) and ad lib fibre fed from the ground or from a low-level container when stabled can prevent these behaviours starting, and can lessen their occurrence in those horses that are already performing them.

It is not solely the mental and physical occupation that does the trick. The head-down posture always has a calming effect on horses, as does the reassuring feeling of some fibrous food constantly present in, and passing through, the gut. The walking/foraging/head-swinging physical movement and mental preoccupation is what horses are programmed to do for about two-thirds to three-quarters of their 24 hours, and such a routine keeps them settled.

What can I do?

- Arrange for as much year-round pasture turnout for your horse as you possibly can, in conditions that will keep him content – with friends, shelter, decent ground conditions, and forage when grass is scarce.
- In the stable, fix up a low-level manger or tub in each corner and fill each one with a different type of short-chopped forage, as well as providing different types of

hay and haylage. Mix additives such as soaked sugar-beet pulp in one, grated carrots in a second, sliced apples in a third, mints and treats in the fourth, and so on. The horse will forage between them all – in the same way that in a more natural outside situation he would choose different grasses -- throughout his stabled hours, and thereby keep interested, busy and appropriately fed.
- This type of feeding should discourage the development of gastric ulcers (see pages 66–7), which, in the same way as hunger, also cause digestive discomfort and pain. Such discomfort is an important contributory factor, along with frustration and acute boredom, to the development of stereotypical behaviour.
- Horse-friendly feeding does reduce the incidence of stereotypies, and can stop them developing in the first place.

REMEMBER

If horses are physically occupied and mentally settled they are far less likely to perform stereotypies of any kind. Other factors apply, but here we are talking feeding.

49 Provide the best possible water supply

Water is the most important nutrient in the feeding spectrum. Many people do not regard water as a nutrient, although it does contain some minerals. A horse's body is around 70 per cent water, so he is more water than anything else. When you consider that in hot weather a working horse – or even one just standing sweating in a hot, muggy stable – can need around 50 litres (13 gallons) of water in one day, its importance is clear.

Ensure the quality of the water supply

Your water supply will probably be under the control of your local water authority and, more immediately, your livery yard proprietor, if applicable. Decades ago, many horses living out had access to natural water supplies such as streams and ponds. As the environment changed, and in particular land management policies and farming and industrial practices, particularly during the latter half of the twentieth century, synthetic chemical products, frequently toxic or even poisonous, often leaked into our land and water courses: ditches, wells, lakes, ponds, streams and rivers. Today, most natural water sources are too risky to rely on for our horses' water because of possible pollution, despite laws aimed at preventing it. Even though, paradoxically, we probably have higher standards of hygiene than our predecessors, expecting everything to be clean and pure, it often isn't. Thus ponds can become stagnant and unusable; a dead and decomposing animal in or near a stream may be contaminating the water and compromising its safety as a water supply downstream; and fertilizers, pesticides, herbicides, insecticides, chemical pollutants and heavy metals such as mercury and lead still get into watercourses despite rules and regulations.

Piped, laid-on mains water is preferred by most people, although water authorities very often, and rather high-handedly, add chemicals such as chlorine and fluoride to our drinking water whether we want them to or not, a practice that is roundly condemned by some medical experts and nutritionists.

What can I do?

- Water can be provided by automatic troughs, or in containers filled by hosepipe. A very inconvenient but sometimes unavoidable way of providing water is to transport it to outlying paddocks in large bowsers.
- However it is supplied, the water container must be safe, with no sharp edges or corners, and as flush as possible with the fence line to minimize the risk of a horse colliding with it, which would very probably cause injury.
- It is, of course, quite possible to have a natural water source analysed fairly frequently, but pollution 'events' can happen overnight, and it is not practicable to have your water checked daily. So it seems that, to be on the safe side, natural water sources should not be relied on, and it is often recommended that they should be fenced off. This does seem a shame, however, where they are also a means of providing pleasure and play for the horses, and in these circumstances you may feel that it is worth taking the chance and using them.
- The only way you can control the quality of mains water is to fit a filter to your supply's main inlet. Many health-conscious people now have filters reducing the quantity of chlorine and fluoride in their household water, and it is possible to do the same for your yard supply.
- Water containers in the stable should have their tops no higher than the horse's elbow for a more natural drinking position. Buckets and tubs are normally placed on the floor, but automatic drinkers are often fixed too high.
- Drinkers with meters are best for checking how much water your horse is, or is not drinking, and a plug in the bottom makes for easier drainage and daily cleaning. Most horses do not like the small wall drinkers meant for cattle, although they will use them if they are really thirsty – but this is not good management. They like large containers with clean, fresh water, and this fact should be given much more attention than it usually is.

CHECK THE WATER SUPPLY FREQUENTLY

Whether your horses are in or out, make sure their supplies are not stagnant and contaminated with algae, particularly blue-green algae, in summer, and rotting leaves, dead birds and animals, or frozen beyond use in winter. Check the supply several times daily because dehydration can occur at any time of year for many reasons, and is a serious health problem.

50 Use purges with care

Older books on horse care recommended the practice of feeding a weekly bran or linseed mash, and of purging horses when they came up from grass for a season's work. For at least a decade, and maybe two, vets and nutritionists have been against this practice as one that constitutes a sudden change in feed content, and therefore bad for the horse's digestion and health. Now some of them are making an about-turn in these areas of horse care and feeding.

What are the supposed benefits of purging?

The horse's large intestine can retain indigestible substances such as soil, sand and grit, lignin (a woody, indigestible fibre), seed husks and generally undigested material, which can build up and lodge in the caecum. The practice of giving a purgative to horses brought up from grass was intended to stimulate bowel movements to 'clean out' the gut and help to expel this debris. The practice was somewhat violent, and horses often suffered a setback in health and took several days and more to recover. Furthermore, once stabled and in work, a weekly bran mash, or bran and linseed mash would be given, as a milder laxative to prevent this build-up; this was normal routine, and it always has been in traditionally run yards.

Over the years scientific research came to the conclusion that the traditional practice of purging in fact did more harm than good to the horse, destroying his gut flora and altogether disrupting his digestive system, and vets, nutritionists and holistic practitioners were against its use. But now some are recommending it again.

What can I do?

First discuss the technicalities with your vet and nutritionist. A clear-out may be advised, but remember that it will upset the microbial population in your horse's gut, so a probiotic and/or prebiotic may be recommended afterwards.

To make a bran mash:

Because bran is low in calcium and high in phosphorus and therefore not good for bone health, do not feed it daily. For a weekly mash you can get small amounts from a pet shop (nearly a feed-bucketful is plenty) so it will not go 'off'. Pour a kettle of boiling water or linseed on it, add a handful of salt, and stir well with a clean stick or wooden spoon. Put a layer of dry bran on top to keep the heat in, wrap it up in old blankets or hay, and let it cook for a few hours. Feed it when it has cooled down enough to stir with your bare hand.

To boil linseed:

Use a cupful of raw seeds per horse, and soak these overnight in cold water. Next day bring to the boil and boil hard for 20 minutes to kill off the poison it is supposed to contain (a moot point, this); then tip it into the bran instead of water, and let it all cook as above. Linseed boils over very easily, so watch it carefully and throw in a good handful of pearl barley to stop it boiling over. A tablespoon of blackstrap molasses (black treacle), too, after boiling makes an irresistible mixture, especially in winter.

HOLISTIC TIP

Rather than go to all the trouble of cooking up linseed and making mashes, a herbalist could prescribe some senna or psyllium for your horse (both natural laxatives), which would probably do the job just as well.

Tack and equipment

The effects of tack and equipment on performance and attitude

The subject of tack and equipment may seem a strange one to put in a book on health, but what we put on our horses certainly constitutes a major part of their care. It can cause a great deal of discomfort, distress and frustration if it does not fit well, is not put on and adjusted properly, or is unsuitable for the horse.

Poor saddle fit is a major cause of pain and distress. Not only does the horse have to move under a girthed-up saddle, but he also has to do so under weight – and that weight may lurch about in an unstable way if the rider is not competent and well balanced, exacerbating any pressure and friction that may already be causing him problems. Furthermore, very often little thought is given to the girth you have put on him: from the saddle you cannot see to what extent it may be digging in behind the elbow when the horse brings his leg back, even though you may realize that he is not 'going forward', or does not seem particularly happy. A girth that is too loose or too tight can cause problems that some riders may not even consider.

Bridles that are too small or too tight – and especially the noseband – can also cause discomfort, even pain, and if too loose they are ineffective. Bits these days are still a source of fascination to many people, but informed knowledge about bitting seems rare, despite there being several excellent books on the subject.

Rugs and blankets often cause more discomfort than most people realize: they are on the horse for many hours at a time, and if badly fitting he has no means of relieving the pain or discomfort other than biting or rubbing at them.

Boots and bandages can restrict the leg action if they rub or have been put on with uneven pressure, or too tightly; and put on too loosely, they can come off or come undone, tripping the horse up and causing injury that way.

Remember: Anything that causes the horse unease of any kind will adversely affect his way of going, either physically due to restriction, or mentally due to fear of causing himself more pain or discomfort if he tries to move normally, or as requested.

On the other hand suitable, well fitting and properly adjusted tack and clothing can only benefit the comfort and safety of both horse and rider, and improve horse care and health.

51 Make the saddle really fit the horse

Saddles can be expensive. I once bought a quality old horse for little more than meat price (remember meat price?), and buying a suitable saddle cost nearly three times as much as the mare herself! But it made a huge difference to her action, comfort and health, because gradually she no longer expected pain and discomfort, and no longer worried about it, and so gave me the thrill of riding her for nearly three years.

How should a saddle really fit?

Because of developments in saddle design, and because more saddlers are now more knowledgeable about fitting them – and also as a result of computerized pressure testing and of equine biomechanics – the skill in designing, making and actually fitting saddles has advanced in leaps and bounds.

The problem with any saddle is that it has to fit both you and your horse, whatever job the horse does, whether jumping, endurance, dressage, showing, hacking or whatever. And if you are uncomfortable, you will not ride well, and this will certainly affect your horse's attitude and performance. And if your horse is uncomfortable he will not go well, and he may even play up, both of which will affect *your* attitude and performance.

Saddles now come not only in a narrow, medium and wide fitting, but also in extra wide, and even wider than that. There are saddles to go on the differently shaped backs of all sorts of different breeds and types of animal: Arabs with flat backs, chunky native ponies, cobs with no withers, Thoroughbreds with high withers, and so on.

The horse must be the first to be fitted, and for this I strongly recommend that you employ a qualified saddle fitter, or a saddler experienced in fitting, to do this job (see pages 84–5).

- The saddle should be symmetrical on both sides (and so should the horse!), and must lie absolutely evenly on the horse's back, with no more pressure in one place than another – no 'bridging', where it presses harder in front and behind because the saddle is flat from front to back and your horse's back isn't; no digging into his back under the cantle; no squeezing the sides of the withers, or pressing on top of them at the front; and so on. Certain retailers may be able to use computerized pads with sensors to check all this.

- Check that the deepest part of the saddle is truly central, mid-way between the pommel and the cantle, and be sure that it remains there when the saddle is girthed up: that is, in the correct place on the horse's back.

- You should be able to fit the side of your hand between the top of the horse's shoulder blade, just below and behind the wither, and the front of the saddle. Most people put saddles on too far forward, which has the effect of tilting the pommel up, the cantle down and, unavoidably, the rider back; this swings the rider's legs forward, and so puts him out of balance. This also hampers the horse's shoulder movement, hindering his action and rocking the saddle (and the rider) slightly from side to side as the top of the shoulder blade swings back at every step.

- The back of the saddle should not extend back beyond the horse's last rib.

- The placement of the stirrup bars also affects the rider's leg position. The ankle bone, or at least the heel,

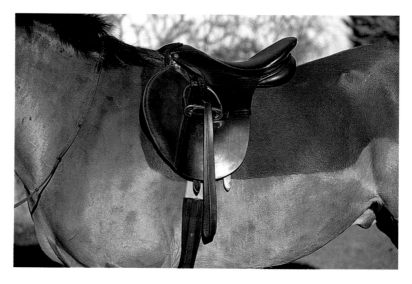

should be directly beneath the seat bones (the bottom of the pelvis), and it is hard to maintain this position if the stirrup bars are too far forward, because they will pull the feet forwards, throwing the rider on to his or her buttocks instead of the seatbones.

- When the horse's heaviest rider is in the saddle, the fitter should be able to slide the flat of four fingers down under the front of the saddle, along under the seat, along the back and round under the cantle, and similarly on the other side, without the obstruction of undue pressure, and without detecting any significant difference in pressure.

- There should be room for three fingers sideways down the gullet of the saddle between the panels; these should be smooth, not lumpy or hard, and not too rounded from side to side: like this they concentrate the pressure in two narrow strips down the horse's back.

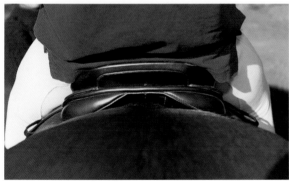

- When the horse is mounted, there should be a clear tunnel of daylight down his back, and the fitter should be able to fit the width of three fingers well down between the pommel and withers when the rider leans forwards.

- If the horse's back is uneven, a skilled fitter and saddler will probably be able to make adjustments to the padding to accommodate this. The problem with the back also needs investigating.

- To see if the saddle fits you, place your hand flat in front of your body on the pommel: it should take the full width of your hand; then place it behind your body at the cantle: again, you should be able to fit the full width of your hand between your seat and the cantle.

- Adjustable-gullet saddles are well worth considering.

And what about numnahs?

Most master saddlers say that a well-fitting saddle does not need a numnah, and point out, rightly, that a numnah under such a saddle makes it too tight, like thick socks inside boots. They say, again rightly, that leather absorbs sweat and the saddle is padded, so why use a numnah? Points taken; however, …

… good modern materials and styles of numnah, pad or saddle cloth do add a resilient cushion for horses that are under saddle for longer periods; they can lift a saddle to allow muscle development in remedial cases; and high-wither styles are ideal for those horses whose numnahs tend to be dragged down on to their withers by their saddles, causing considerable pressure. Many materials from the most simple to the most high-tech are available.

Try your horse with and without a numnah or other pad, and see how he goes, and whether there are signs of uneven sweating, pressure (lumps shortly after removing the saddle) or friction (rubbed hair). You could also consult a saddle fitter and/or physiotherapist for their opinion.

The Western saddle

There are probably as many types of Western saddle as there are English, all of them based on the requirement of a long working day herding cattle, necessitating comfort; but some are now specialized for Western sports such as barrel racing, pleasure riding, reining, and so on.

How did the Western saddle evolve?

The predecessors of the Western saddle came to America with the conquistadors in the sixteenth century: their Iberian saddles were a mixture of mediaeval European knights' saddles and Moorish styles from the Moorish occupation of Iberia. These saddles were mainly used for war, but they were also used for cattle herding, and so the security and comfort of the rider was paramount: therefore high pommels and cantles and padding were used.

In Mexico and the western states of what is now the USA, cattle ranching was the way of life, and different methods developed according to the local terrain, necessitating slightly different saddle designs.

How do Western saddles differ from English ones?

Apart from being much more decorative, with embossing and metal fittings, the Western saddle covers much more of the horse and is heavier, although lighter ones are now made for sport and smaller animals. The bearing surface under the seat spreads the weight better (given good fit), although older ones do still tilt the rider towards the cantle, like the old knights' saddles. Western saddles do not have adjustable or spring trees.

To enhance comfort for the horse the saddle is normally placed over folded blankets, which doubled as a bed-roll for the cowboy. The stirrup leathers, called fenders, are wide in order to protect the rider's legs from sweat, and the stirrups may be wood covered with rawhide to maintain a moderate temperature, something that is not possible with metal. There are various designs aimed at comfort and protection.

The front arch of a roping saddle is strengthened with steel to take the enormous strain of a steer pulling on the pommel horn, it is widened to protect the horse's shoulders, and it has padded shoulders, or 'swells', to help prevent the rider being unseated forwards as the steer jerks on the rope. Roping also necessitates two girths, or cinches, called 'double rigging': the front one is fairly tight, and the back one is looser, only coming into action when the saddle is pulled forwards by the steer.

Modern Western saddles may be very ornate, and are lighter and neater than the originals; they are of different designs according to region and purpose. In particular, the seats do not slope so steeply backwards, often only one cinch is used (single rigging), and the stirrups are placed further back to accommodate better balanced riding.

Fitting a modern Western saddle:
Usually a lighter blanket is needed, as today's saddles are designed to fit more exactly. A wide tree can be made acceptable by thicker blankets, provided these do not cause the saddle to roll from side to side. As with an English saddle, adding pads underneath to prevent a narrow tree pinching in fact only makes it tighter. Again as with an English saddle, the saddle must not press anywhere on the withers or backbone, or interfere with the shoulders, or press on the loins.

52 Risers and pads: a temporary solution to saddle fit

Horses change in condition and shape throughout the year according to their prevailing lifestyle. Some saddles can be adjusted accordingly, but most can't, so we try to pad them up in various ways. Some horses are difficult to fit, too, so we try different devices to help – but maybe without understanding the full effects of what we're doing.

Can back risers and wither pads improve fit?

In certain circumstances pads and risers improve saddle fit, but they should be regarded as temporary solutions. Nothing is as good as a saddle that fits properly, and is designed for the kind of riding you want to do. (Also read pages 84 and 85.)

- If you have a horse/saddle combination where the front of the saddle is lower than the back, or the saddle presses on the withers, you'll be considering a riser to lift it. But before you do, look where the deepest part of the seat is. If it is central and you use a pommel riser, you will tilt the saddle up and back so the deepest point moves back, pulling the rider towards the cantle and placing pressure on the back under it. If the deepest part of the seat is nearer the pommel, as in some jumping saddles, a riser may help to balance the saddle for flatwork, but the stirrup bars may be too far forward for flatwork, pulling the legs forwards.

- If the problem is pressure on top of the withers, a riser or wither pad could help; but again, check the seat shape, and also the width of the pommel arch, because if the sides of the withers are pinched, no pad or riser can help because it will make the saddle tighter still. With a high-withered horse, consider using a full high-withers backpad plus a pommel riser on top of it under the pommel to raise it all up, depending on the seat position.

- A common problem today is the flat-panelled saddle (from front to back), usually synthetic, that presses down beneath the pommel and the cantle but 'bridges' the centre of the back. This also happens with a sway-backed horse. Putting a pad in the middle over a numnah may spread the pressure and provide a good temporary solution.

- Finally, consider the croup-high horse where everything slides forwards and down. A pad and/or riser in front can help correct the directional pull, but again, watch out that a good central seat dip is not tilted backwards.

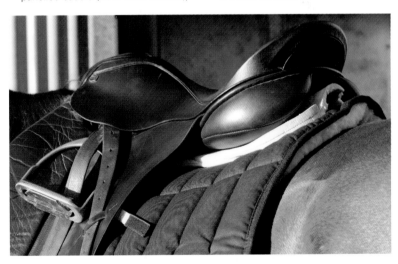

53 Choose the right saddle for optimum performance

Saddles are made for several different jobs, and a good one will be balanced accordingly. If you want to jump seriously high fences then it's no good using a dressage saddle, or using a show saddle if you want to do endurance rides. Understanding how a saddle functions, sandwiched between your horse and yourself, is a great help.

What do I need to consider?

Saddles are made on a framework called the tree: it dictates the shape, fit and best use of the saddle. The lower ends of the front arch (pommel) are called the tree points and need to be sufficiently wide or narrow to fit your horse (allowing for covering padding) without either pinching (too narrow) or rocking (too wide). The stirrup bars, which obviously take much of the weight of the rider, are fixed behind, but fairly near the points, depending on design, so in a too-narrow saddle or one that is insufficiently padded, or where the padding has compressed from use, concentrated pressure and possible pain is felt by the horse just below and behind the withers from these two structures.

At the other end of the saddle -- the back arch or cantle -- incorrectly balanced or badly fitting saddles will rub, digging in particularly under riders who sit heavily, and will flop up and down during movement if the panels do not align with the horse's back.

Today, more saddlers, saddle fitters and riders increasingly understand the need for the rider's ankles/ heels to fall easily beneath his/her seatbones for balanced, effective riding, whether jumping or on the flat; and the better the riding, the more comfortable the horse, and the better altogether for his overall health and well-being. The two extremes of saddle design for sport riding nowadays are those for show-jumping and dressage.

The modern jumping saddle Nowadays this sort of saddle may not have as forward cut a flap as its immediate predecessors, but it still needs to accommodate the shorter stirrup and more bent, forward knee position that is needed to negotiate higher fences. The stirrup bars on specialist jumping saddles are often set well forward, and

very close to the points of the saddle tree; but a balanced jumping seat still demands that the lower leg remains more or less vertical with the toe beneath the knee, so remaining stable enough to allow the rider to fold down, not forwards, over the jump, even over wide spreads, pushing the seat back a little. Puissance jumps need a different technique.

The dressage saddle This type of saddle has the stirrup bar set further back to accommodate the longer leg position, with the ankle/heel held effortlessly beneath the seat bones. This facilitates the dressage seat in which an onlooker could, from the side, drop a vertical line from the rider's ear, through the shoulder, hip and heel.

The everyday saddle For everyday riding in any discipline at a moderate level probably the best option would be a working hunter or very-slightly-dressage-cut saddle. Most modern general purpose (GP) saddles are nearer to jumping saddles in their cut. There are also specialist-designed saddles with air-filled or floating panels, no trees, half trees and adjustable front arches; these are well worth investigating.

Does it matter what kind of girth I use?

Choice of girth is important. The Atherstone and other girths cut back behind the elbows give real freedom for the elbows. Elastic inserts at both ends help the horse to breathe freely. Girths with an insert at only one end 'give' only at that end when the horse breathes in, so the saddle tilts sideways towards the fixed end, then back again – not good for the horse's back, the saddle, or the rider's balance. With any girth, you should be able to slide the four fingers of your hand between girth and horse when it is tightened.

54 Consult a saddle fitter

The ancient craft of saddle and harness making has always had to be progressive to a certain degree. Today, with the increasing interest in equine comfort and efficiency, saddle designs continue to be forward-looking according to the demands of the market and of riding technique. Now there are saddle fitters as well.

What is the difference between a saddler and a saddle fitter?

We assume that saddlers will be able to fit saddles, so why the need for a saddle fitter? For thousands of years saddlers have fitted saddles and harness to horses. It takes years to become a competent saddler, and much of the work and skill involves the technique of actually making the saddle, bridle or harness – so many stitches to the inch, specific lining and padding materials, tooling, various metals for buckles, choosing leather for particular purposes. As part of their training and work, saddlers are trained to fit saddles.

So, the difference between a saddler and a saddle fitter is that a saddler is as involved with the skills of making saddles, bridles and harness as he is to fitting them to his clients' horses, whereas a saddle fitter is a specialist in the fitting of saddles. He or she may or may not also be a saddler.

Training and qualifications

In the UK, a foundation course in saddle fitting is run by the British Equestrian Trade Association and the Society of Master Saddlers together. This is a basic introduction to the principles of saddle fitting, and helps fitters to follow a set procedure so that they get a system to work to. The course is open almost exclusively to members of BETA and/or SMS and involves mainly saddlery retailers. However, equestrian professionals such as veterinary surgeons, chartered physiotherapists, chiropractors, registered farriers, those with the BHSI or FBHS qualification, and others at the discretion of the organizers, may also take the course if places are available.

The foundation course is a two-day course involving classroom and practical work. Students study basic equine biomechanics and the horse's skeleton, the way a saddle affects movement, the different types of saddles, and finally saddle construction, and how the design and construction affects and fits the horse. This course is not a qualification as such, but on completion, students receive a certificate of attendance.

Possession of the certificate enables the student to go on to take the SMS five-day saddle-fitting course involving four days of teaching, and two months later, one day of student assessment when several horses must be fitted with different saddles. For successful students this results in a professional, industry-recognized qualification and entry into the SMS saddle fitters' register.

Applicants for the SMS five-day course must be in full-time employment with a fully paid-up member of the society, or be a member in their own right. They need at least three years' experience in saddle fitting, and must have attended the foundation course.

So far not every saddlery retailer can boast a qualified saddle fitter on its staff, but the situation is improving.

How can they help me choose the right saddle?

Most saddle fitters, qualified or otherwise, work for a retail saddler and deal with individual clients, fitting both new and second-hand saddles in their employer's stock, and assessing saddles taken in part exchange. They can also do minor adjustments to saddles.

A saddle requiring something more major will normally be taken to the retailer's premises and altered by a saddler or qualified fitter.

SPECIALIST SADDLES

Saddles of specialist design such as, in the UK, the Reactorpanel range, the Cair range, the Balance saddling system, Wow saddles and others, will require fitters specifically trained to fit those types of saddle according to those systems.

55 Use the simplest equipment for the happy horse

The range of horse tack and equipment is so vast these days that it is quite understandable that many people feel they 'should' have more gear than they do: maybe they are missing out on some wondrous piece of tack that will solve all their problems. Some items are good and useful, a few risk being too coercive, and of course, any item of tack can be positively harmful if not used sympathetically by the trainer.

What am I aiming at in my riding?

Many years ago I watched two displays that have truly been my inspiration ever since. One was by a small riding school with a team of exuberant horses, bareback and with only cords through their mouths, ridden without whips or spurs, and doing what they obviously did regularly for fun. The other was the classical Portuguese maestro Nuno Oliveira at Wembley in the 1960s. These skilled riders used the simplest of equipment, and the horses were joyful, light, and naturally balanced, showing under human direction what they could do naturally.

Only *you* know what you are aiming at in your riding,

but if you care about your horse, then you care about the effect your riding has on him. Maybe you think about him as he is in nature, and so perhaps your aim is to try to preserve his natural spirit under saddle and in partnership with you. I cannot think of any better.

How can I achieve this?

- Xenophon, the famous ancient Greek cavalry commander, was surely not the first human to treat the horse as a living, feeling being, and to realize that it gave of its best when humanely and fairly treated. Most horses (agreed, not all) want to please, partly because they know instinctively that this will ensure their acceptance among those who appear to be the basis of their herd.

- A true horseman may have ulterior motives in his riding (a superb hack, an exhilarating 'feel', an Olympic medal), but so long as a horse is truly cared about and nurtured, he will usually do his best to achieve what he thinks we want (and it's up to us to get through to him) without either gadgets or equipment.

- In the course of my teaching I sometimes come across seemingly horrendous problems and horses loaded down with gear, the latest bit ideas, expensive saddles -- and riders still not sure as to what equipment to use. Much equipment is still bought because another owner on the yard has recommended it, or an advert they read sounded particularly convincing.

- I usually remove most of the 'gear' and try to get to the root of the problem, recommending a well-fitting and correctly placed saddle and a simple, comfortable bit. Very often this involves lowering bits, loosening nosebands, pushing saddles back, loosening girths, and relaxing the rider.

- A comfortable horse is a happy horse; if he is relaxed in mind, body and attitude he will be easier to ride, and this can only mean a healthier horse, more likely to thrive and develop a long partnership with his rider.

56 Train if you plan to use restrainer or pressure halters

A horse is a formidable animal to control if he is not well behaved. At about half a ton/tonne in weight, with an instinctive fear of being restrained and an impulse to flee rather than think in times of perceived danger, it is no wonder that some owners welcome anything that will help them to control a 'situation', whether or not they really understand how it works.

What exactly are restrainer or pressure halters?

There are several different designs of these halters, but all of them have two things in common:

1 They are not normally meant for tying up a horse.

2 They should be used on a 'check and release' system, and never with sustained pressure.

Most are made out of rounded, braided rope, not flat straps, and are put on in such a way that if you pull on the leadrope, the halter will tighten around the horse's head. Some types have knots in the rope in strategic places, which it is claimed accord with various acupressure points on the head: when subjected to pressure from the knots, the effect is said to quieten the horse down.

These halters operate on the basis of tightening on the horse's head and causing him discomfort when he does something we don't want him to do, and of the discomfort being removed by the pressure being released the instant he complies with what we want. The principle is the same as that of natural equine communication, where a nip, bite or kick (a short, sharp and uncomfortable sensation) means 'go away' or 'stop it'. When the offender retreats or stops being a nuisance, the biting stops.

Thus if a horse is misbehaving in hand – won't lead, jinks about, rears and so on – he is given a short, sharp jerk on the leadrope by the handler, followed immediately by its release, and maybe another jerk if the bad behaviour continues. The horse's reward for good behaviour is that the jerks stop.

This works well as long as the halter is used correctly. If, however, a sustained pull and very rough jerks are used, they can cause pain and injury, and lead to a lot of behavioural problems. You can see how dangerous these effects would be if a horse were tied up in such a halter and pulled back, as some do.

Should I get a restrainer halter for my horse?

If your horse behaves badly and you feel such a halter would help the situation, contact a professional trained in the use of such a halter, for instance someone from the Intelligent Horsemanship Association. They will train your horse and also teach you how to use the halter in future.

57 Find the right bit for your horse

There are innumerable bits of different design on the market today. In the last twenty years traditional bits, both common and obscure, have been added to, with newer designs, theories, ranges, and whole, often complex, bitting systems. How do you know which is best for your particular horse?

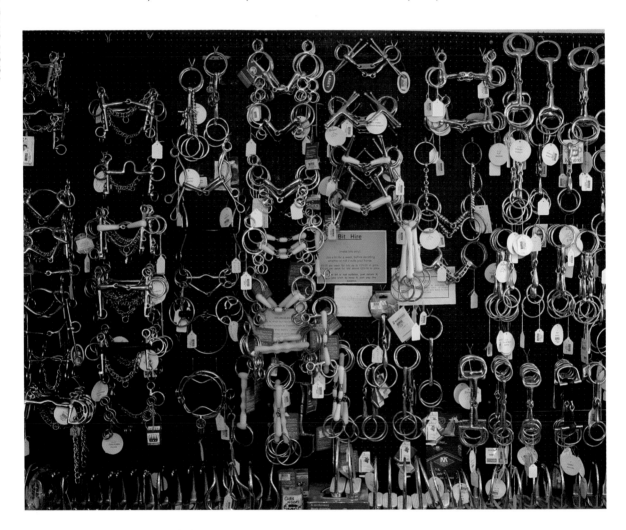

Things to consider

The best bit for your horse is the one in which he goes most kindly, and in which he is controllable – even though this may not be the one you have worked out would be best for him! The word 'controllable' may sound as though the bit is the main means of 'forcing' a horse to do what you want, whereas anyone with much experience at all knows that it is extremely difficult to force a horse to do anything using normal means. A skilled rider with an amenable horse will not use the bit to stop, but the mind, upper body and seat,

perhaps with a very slight feel on the reins or maybe just a change of hand position.

It has to be said, though, that not all horses are amenable despite good schooling and a happy relationship with their rider: some sometimes just lose their 'cool', and some think that they always know best, even though they are normally biddable. For safety's sake, such horses need to accept a means of control and guidance, and finding a bit that they both accept and respect is essential for safety. This makes for a happier horse and a more rewarding partnership.

Factors affecting the choice of a bit

- We hear a lot about studying the make and shape of your horse's mouth, but over the years I have found that only occasionally is anything required other than a French link snaffle, which fits over the tongue and jaw more comfortably than a single joint, or a simple mullen-mouthed (half-moon) pelham. Not all horses like a double bridle.

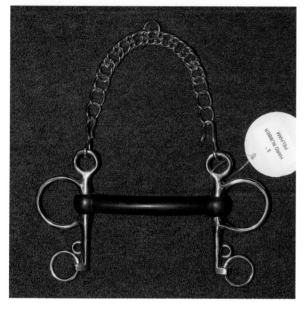

- Try a loose-ring snaffle for a horse that does not move his bit around or use it much, and an eggbutt for one with the opposite problem, of too much movement or fussing.
- The material from which the bit is made also affects whether or not the horse likes it. Copper and other metals or plastics with various tastes may cause a reaction in the mouth that produces saliva, and this gives the possibly false impression that the horse likes them. Remember that he has no choice, and we cannot know how it tastes

to him. It is probably best to keep to stainless steel, which is tasteless (although some horses go better in vulcanite or rubber-covered bits), and to provide a pleasant taste, if required, by giving a mint or some other treat before and/ or after putting the bit in.

- The idea has grown up that the more froth the horse makes, the better – it makes for a 'soft mouth', they say. In fact, excessive frothing and drooling indicates distress in mammals, including horses, and a very 'dry' mouth can indicate actual fear. What we need is the in-between state of a slightly wet mouth, and a confident, moderate playing with the bit, not a rigid hold or constant champing.
- The idea that a thick mouthpiece is 'kind' may also be a fallacy, and many horses with small mouths prefer a slimmer one. Research in Canada by Dr Hilary Clayton showed that there is rarely any excess space in a horse's mouth for a bit. Also, she showed that the tongue takes almost all the pressure from the mouthpiece of even a moderately ported bit. It is mobile and strong, and horses are skilled at pushing the bit around with it, even with a closed mouth.
- For your horse to be comfortable, ignore the present trend for bits to be fitted too high: this does not make for more control, but causes discomfort and sometimes pain from stretched and even cracked skin that can become infected. A jointed snaffle should create *one* wrinkle at the corners of the mouth or, at most if the tushes are in the way, two. Straight-bar/mullen-mouth bits should just touch the corners, and the curb of a double bridle should not touch them at all, lying about 1cm or ½in below the bridoon, which rests over the top of it.
- Correct width is important in order to prevent pinching or uncomfortable sliding about. You should be able to fit the width of one finger between the bit cheek and the face on one side.
- A curb chain of any material should lie well down in the chin/curb groove, not part-way up the jawbones where it can really hurt. Shorten it so that it comes into operation when the bit cheek is at 45 degrees to the line of the lips.

HOLISTIC TIP

Keep it simple. Remember the old saying: 'Most bits are made for men's minds, not horses' mouths.' The skill and sensitivity of the hands on the other end of the reins are far more important than the bit.

58 Use the simplest training aid possible

There are many schooling aids on the market and most seem to be misused, despite the various sources of information that explain how to use them. They are all aimed at making schooling easier, and bringing results more quickly -- but if they are used wrongly they can actually ruin your horse's way of going, not enhance it, and badly affect his attitude to you and his work.

Which aid should I choose?

All these aids are aimed at teaching a horse to go correctly, with his back and belly up, his hindquarters and legs tilted under and pushing, and his head and neck pushed forwards and somewhat down, with his nose in front of the vertical. If you really feel that you need a training aid to achieve this, the 'best' is the one that you find simplest to use and which your horse accepts most happily, whilst at the same time it produces the right result. A teacher who empathizes with you and your horse and does not try to force results is a tremendous help in this situation.

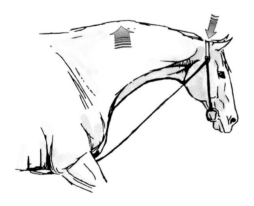

Some aids aim to work on the horse's forehand *and* hindquarters; others, such as the traditional Chambon (above) or de Gogue, influence only the forehand and head and neck, with the view that the horse gets the idea and comes into a correct posture of his own accord. Some are for use under saddle, and others only on the unridden horse.

What should I do?

- Remember that the whole point of using a training aid is to teach the horse to use and develop his own muscles so that he acquires the strength to work correctly without it.
- Any device that enables or obliges him to 'lean' on it or to resist it – such as a too-short standing martingale – or

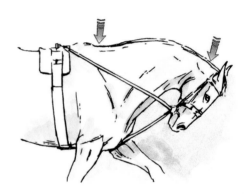

draw-reins or running-reins that are used to pull his head in (above), or whole-body devices adjusted to force him into an outline -- encourages and maybe forces him to use the wrong muscles, and can even cause soft tissue injury.
- Avoid any instructor who favours these techniques.
- Consider that when a wrongly used aid is removed, the horse may go even worse than he did before, because it has not encouraged correct muscle use and posture, but has developed the horse incorrectly, and so he finds it more difficult to work correctly than he did before.

59 Check the fit of your rugs

Despite the best of intentions on the part of the owner or carer, clothing can be the bane of a horse's life. From my observations, I am sure that most horses would feel more comfortable without their rugs, temperature notwithstanding. Badly used clothing can be a health hazard, mainly from overloading and incorrect fit.

Our reasons for using rugs, blankets and sheets

Clothing can be regarded as a form of portable shelter: it protects the horse from his environment to some extent, from insects, sun, heat, cold, wet and wind. Some horses wear clothing a lot of the time, even all the time depending on circumstances – and some owners overlook the importance of comfort and fit. Imagine spending nearly all your life wearing clothes that feel awful, that pull, rub, irritate or even hurt you.

The two key factors about clothing are these:

1 Use it only when necessary: many people use too much of it, and too often (see page 45).
2 Only use clothing that does not rub, irritate and potentially injure your horse – in other words, only use clothing that fits correctly.

The main elements of good fit

Rugs are much better made today and are generally horse-shaped with space-makers for movement – but not all. You can get a rug that is the perfect size but not the perfect shape (fit) for your horse. These 'fitting facts' apply whether we are talking about summer or winter rugs:

- The top of the neckline should come well in front of the withers, and the top of the back edge should reach the root of the tail, going a little past it in outdoor rugs.
- The neckline itself should fit up around the base of the neck like a collar, not come down on to the shoulders where it will rub and pull, and can actually cause a permanent change for the worse in the horse's action.
- The front fastenings should be designed (maybe in a V-shape) to enable the horse to get his head down to graze and root in comfort and without pulling the rug down on to his withers.
- The back seam, if there is one, should be undulating to suit the horse's back.

- The bottom edge should come just past the elbows and stifles, longer in an outdoor rug.
- There should be a fuller cut at the shoulders and stifles, or shaping pleats or darts, to allow for really free movement of the shoulders, hips and legs, so making for both fit and real freedom. This is extremely important. It is the shoulders and withers that are susceptible to most of the pressure and rubbing.

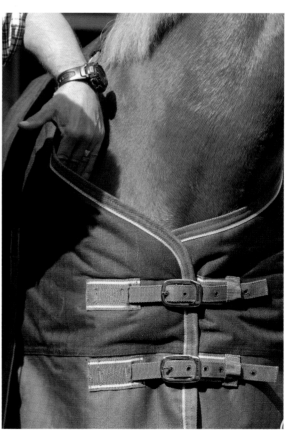

NO REMEDY FOR BAD FIT

Using liners and padding to prevent rubbing will not improve a rug's fit. Rather make sure rugs fit properly and don't burden your horse with extra gear.

60 Understand the use of exercise boots and bandages

The horse's legs are very thinly protected by skin and are therefore extremely vulnerable to injury, both from wounds and also strains and sprains. Their complex arrangement of muscles (in their upper parts), tendons and sheaths, ligaments, bones and joints is a miracle of natural engineering. How can we best protect them?

The advantages and disadvantages of leg protection

We hear a lot about supporting horses' legs, by which is usually meant helping the tendons and ligaments to withstand the stresses and strains put upon them during the often extreme work we demand of them, as opposed to that they would experience in nature.

The only way you can support a horse's lower leg during movement is to more or less restrict the flexing action of the fetlock joint, because it is the extreme flexion of this joint, where the ergot very often actually touches the ground as in galloping and jumping, that puts maximal tension on the tendons and ligaments.

- To offer at least some support with exercise/work bandages, you must bandage (over padding) under the fetlock, bringing the bandage turns up above the angle of the joint in front to avoid pressure there. Bandages must be put on very evenly, and fastened by means of Velcro, strong safety pins, wide tape such as masking or adhesive tape, or by sewing them on. Ordinary attached tapes are risky because of uneven pressure, which can also occur during bandaging. It is a skilled job, but it can be learnt.

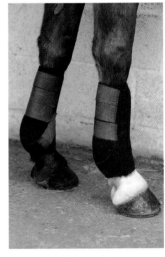

- Work boots that offer support – a claim backed up by scientific studies and reports – are a safer and more effective choice than 'ordinary' work boots. Otherwise, all your horse will get from boots is protection from impact (interfering and knocks) – though this is still worthwhile, of course. Support boots have a strap under the fetlock, and its positioning is crucial. If they are new to you, you should certainly have a demonstration, and perhaps an individual fitting, from the supplier or someone who is experienced in their use.

What should I do?

Some boots are now made of material that allows heat to escape: it is known that if the core temperature of a tendon rises, injury is more likely, so it is best to keep the legs cool. This is one reason I would only use boots for work not exercise; the other is to give the legs a chance to function and strengthen normally, without the changing pressures on the tendons exerted by boots and bandages.

61 Let your horse travel in safety and comfort

Travelling can be a risky business for horses. They are trusting passengers inside the vehicle, which takes them they know not where, when anything can happen. Wearing suitable protective equipment, and taking other precautions, can lessen the chances of injury and illness.

What sort of injury can horses incur?

The risks start as soon as you even begin loading up. Slips and trips can happen to the best traveller, if something alarms the horse as he is loading he can throw up his head and bang it on the roof, he can slip on the ramp, trip up, kick himself or cut a leg. During the trip he may be swung around corners and lurched about by inconsiderate driving so he treads on himself or knocks his lower legs on the bottom of the partitions. He may sit hard on the breeching bar, scraping and bruising his tail, or he may sweat up.

What equipment should I use?

- Padded, all-in-one travelling boots to protect the legs; failing these, you will need stable bandages put on over padding.
- Knee pads, hock boots and over-reach boots on all four feet.
- A reinforced poll guard.
- A tail bandage to protect the tail, maybe under a tail guard if the horse is wearing a rug to which to fasten it.
- A rug or sheet depending on the weather. Check the ventilation,

and consider the time of year and whether or not your horse is clipped or prone to sweating up, and then rug accordingly, or not at all.

Is there anything else to consider?

- Most horses travel best tail-to-the-engine, preferably herringbone fashion with the tail towards the driver and the head towards the roadside. It should be possible to have horseboxes converted like this, but trailers need to be specially designed for it because of the altered weight distribution.
- It is also essential for all but short trips for the horse to be able to get his head down for airway drainage. Bacterial infection quickly builds up in the enclosed atmosphere of a vehicle, causing 'shipping fever': hence the need for good ventilation without draughts. Tying horses to a ring level with the wither allows them to do this whereas tying up next to the head, especially too short, does not, and can make many horses feel very insecure and so prone to stress and colic, and to muscle tension that prevents them balancing properly.
- Top tip: drive as if you had no brake. This really steadies you up.

The healthy hoof

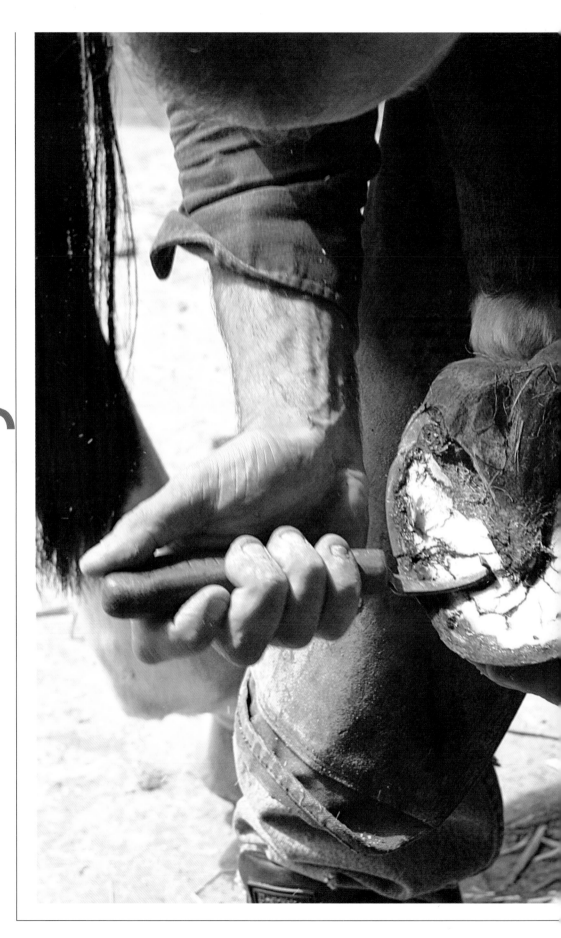

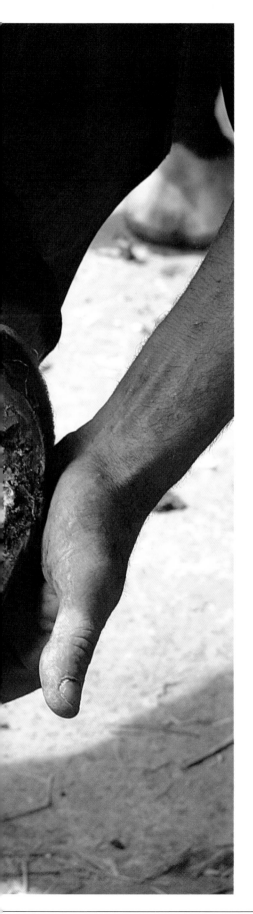

Farriery and the healthy hoof

The farrier is an essential member of the management team of any horse, whether in work or resting. The first foot protection for horses seems to have consisted of plaited rope boots, then tough leather boots that were still in use in the most recent of the ancient civilizations, that of Rome. Tie-on metal sandals preceded shoes, and it is likely that nailed-on shoes probably began to appear no earlier than around 400BC in the Celtic civilization. It seems amazing that none of the great and learned civilizations before then thought of it.

It is only in the last twenty years or so, however, that any significant advances have taken place in trimming and shoeing horses' feet, although the invention of studs a few decades ago, mainly as equestrianism began to grow as a sport, made a big difference to horses expected to work in all ground conditions, and to the work of the farrier who no longer had to make shoes with features such as calkins and wedges to give horses the necessary security.

All those concerned for the welfare of their horses appreciate the necessity of keeping their horses' feet regularly and frequently trimmed, and shod where appropriate; but there are many others who cut back on the significant cost of farriery for reasons of economy, often to the great detriment of their horse's feet, and therefore also to his comfort, security and confidence. In fact there is no real way to cut back on farriery costs and safeguard the health of your horse's feet: if your horse needs shoes, he needs shoes, and even if he doesn't, his feet will need properly and regularly trimming and balancing in accordance with his own foot conformation and action.

Synthetic and rubber shoes have been tried over the years, and can help various foot problems. However, at the time of writing, the author does not know of a viable synthetic alternative to metal shoes for strenuous athletic work.

62 Recognize the farrier's essential role

Farriers, whether they realize it or not, are a regular topic of conversation among horse owners, for better and for worse! For most owners it is clearly impossible to keep a horse going without their services, but some find it very hard indeed to establish a happy relationship. Is there a solution?

What makes a farrier?

Until about a hundred years ago, farriers also worked regularly as veterinary surgeons, performing all sorts of operations and treatments on horses, not necessarily on their hooves, a proceeding that would be unheard of now. Today there is a very clear distinction between the two professions – but farriers still often work closely with vets.

To become a farrier today the prospective student must complete an Advanced Modern Apprenticeship lasting four years and two months, involving college study and working with a registered farrier. At the end of that time, the successful student is awarded the Diploma of the Worshipful Company of Farriers (DipWCF), which enables him or her to be registered with the Farriers Registration Council as a person competent to shoe horses. Higher qualifications that may be taken subsequently are the Associateship of the Worshipful Company of Farriers (AWCF) and the Fellowship of the Worshipful Company of Farriers (FWCF).

The register also accepts farriers who were working before the Farriers (Registration) (Amendment) Act 1977 became effective in 1980, but who do not have qualifications. Anyone who is not on the register at all may not legally shoe horses or trim the feet of horses not their own. Horse owners may, though, trim their own horses' feet provided that they do not intend to shoe those horses.

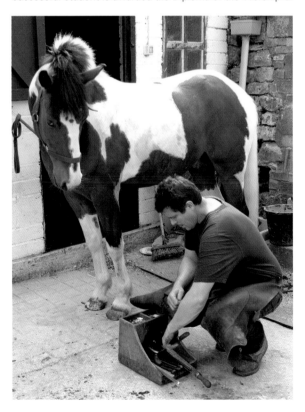

What else should be considered?

The fact that a farrier is registered should ensure an acceptable level of competence in his craft, but it is also important that farriers and horse owners have a reasonable working relationship with each other, too.

Word of mouth is by far the most usual means of finding a farrier; pertinent questions to ask other horse owners might be:

- Does your farrier turn up?
- Does he return phone messages?
- Do the shoes stay on?
- Is he easy to talk to about your horse's needs, new developments, and so on?
- Does he have a Professional attitude? (Note the capital P!)
- Is he rough with your horse?
- Does he appear to do a good job?

No human (or horse) is perfect, of course, but your farrier is an extremely important person in the life of both you and your horse, so it's worth taking the trouble to try and get it right.

63 Be fair to your farrier

A farrier's job is hard, risky, difficult and dirty – and above all, skilful. Farriers are out in all weathers, and almost always on a tight schedule. As well as a busy routine work schedule, they will often have emergencies to attend to, they can be ill, they like a holiday now and then and, unless they have a 'static' forge, their van can break down and cause problems. What can you do to help?

Don't be a difficult client

A farrier I had years ago used to agree with me that most farriers are slightly mad. 'We have to be,' he said, 'to spend so much time bent double around the back end of a horse being s*** on for crumpence.' Mad or not, we all need to get on with our farrier, so here is a list of a dozen Don'ts for horse owners:

Don't:
- Expect your farrier to catch your horse and bring him in.
- Neglect to pick out his feet between visits (out of sight, out of mind).
- Ring your farrier late at night and demand that he comes next day because your horse has lost a shoe – and they've only been on three months.
- Present your horse with wet and, even better, muddy legs and feet – he'll really love this.
- Tell your farrier exactly how you want your horse trimmed and shod, and even how to do it – he'll love this even more.
- Offer him a dark box to work in, with stinky bedding and full of clutter.
- Expect him to shoe your horse in the rain while you stand under cover drinking coffee – and don't offer him any.
- Stand elsewhere chatting to your friends.
- If your horse is bad to tie up, tie him up and leave him, rather than holding him.
- Ask your farrier if you can pay next time, or send the money on.
- Forget to show appreciation, or even to say thank you.
- Omit to book another appointment.

What can I do to help?

Alternatively, here are several things you must be sure to do in order to preserve a happy relationship with your farrier:

Do:
- Have your horse in and ready on time, with clean, dry feet and legs.
- Have somewhere amenable for him to work in, under cover if necessary, well lit and with a clean, clear floor area.
- Make sure that your horse is as well behaved as possible. Get expert help to accustom him to shoeing, if necessary.
- If your horse has a problem or is tricky to shoe due to, say, joint problems or previous rough treatment, ask your farrier to allow for it. (Some older horses benefit from a couple of days of phenybutazone before and after farriery.)
- Be present yourself, or designate a trustworthy person.
- Offer your farrier somewhere to wash and dry his hands, if at all possible.
- Show appreciation and gratitude.
- Pay when your horse is shod, in cash or with a cheque that won't bounce.
- Book again when you pay.

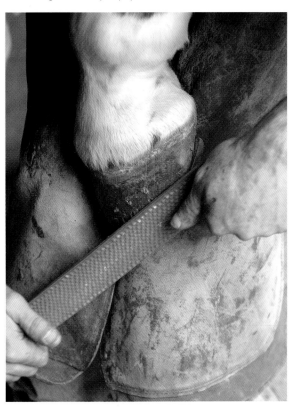

64 Learn from your farrier

We can read books and articles on farriery, study different shoes and their probable effects and so on, but there's nothing quite like the practical experience of watching your farrier shoe your particular horse, with all his individual quirks, for learning about his specific needs.

How does the lay person learn about farriery?

Reading good books and articles by people who know what they're talking about is excellent for learning about the theories and practices of trimming and shoeing horses. Then watch it being put into practice by a good working farrier, and/or discuss it with him. It may be well worthwhile paying a farrier for his time (they're always frantically busy) if there is a problem or an issue that you would like explaining, or to discuss new ideas, or to clear up a confusing point.

What can I do?

When your farrier is shoeing your horse he is obviously concentrating on his job, but even the busiest farrier will appreciate your taking an interest in his work, and having an enquiring mind about farriery in general. It's his profession and his life's work, after all, and most are disappointed at the lack of interest and knowledge shown by many horse owners. (Some are less forthcoming in this respect, but they are in the minority.) So don't be afraid to ask him why he trims and shoes your horse in the way he does; tell him what you understand of the problem, and ask for his opinion.

Furthermore, if your vet has recommended particular treatment for your horse's hooves, ask your farrier what he thinks; and if their proposed treatments differ, tactfully ask him if the two of them will be discussing it;

and if they are, ask if they might bring you into their consultations. There is no room for professional pride when the wellbeing of an animal is at stake.

Formerly, vets and farriers

seemed wary of each other but now there is much more widespread co-operation between the two professions and also mutual respect.

65 Establish the 'perfect' farrier/client relationship

If you know your farrier quite well you will already know what to expect from him. So let's imagine you have a new farrier, you have booked him to come and shoe your horse on word-of-mouth recommendation and because he's a registered professional.

The problems he faces

Horses are unpredictable, extremely strong, quick-thinking animals who don't reason like humans, and because of this they can be potentially dangerous to us. Your farrier knows this, but he doesn't know your horse. Therefore, if he seems over-careful when handling your horse, it's not because he's incompetent, it's because he is self-employed and has to take care of himself and maybe his family because no one else will.

His next problem is you: he doesn't know what kind of person you are, either, how much you know, how much you care, whether you are competent to handle and look after your own horse, and whether or not you will pay up promptly and without quibble when he has finished the job.

An ideal situation

The 'perfect' farrier will turn up on time (or he will have rung beforehand to say he's running late). Your horse will be ready and waiting, with clean, dry legs and feet, and will be well behaved for shoeing (since you are the 'perfect' client).

- He will spend a bit of time talking to your horse and studying his attitude.
- He will pick up all four feet and examine the wear pattern on each; he will know from this how the horse moves -- although he should ask you to walk and trot him up anyway.
- He should ask what kind of work you do with your horse, and discuss his findings and recommendations, and ask your opinions. Only then will he start work.

- First he will remove the shoes, check the condition of the horn, pointing out any problems, tell you what he plans to do, and choose suitable shoes from his stock.
- He will trim the feet and shoe them, either hot or cold, shaping the shoes to fit the feet, not burning them on too long to 'make a bed' but just touching them on lightly; he will then nail them on, clench up, not rasping the wall too much, and maybe finish with a hoof dressing.
- He will expect you to hold, handle and control your horse competently. If your horse misbehaves and you can't cope he will either soothe him if the horse is genuinely worried, or correct him, firmly but not brutally.
- He will not hold any leg in an exaggeratedly flexed, abducted (outward) or very uncomfortable position: a fine line needs to be drawn here, but sometimes a horse just has to put a foot down if he is to relieve severe discomfort, or even stay on his feet. A good farrier will understand this and hold the foot lower and closer to the body in a more natural, comfortable position. This is perfectly possible: you probably do it every day when you pick his feet out and check his shoes.
- (The foundation for horses becoming difficult to shoe is laid by owners who contribute by not training and properly handling and disciplining them. However, a farrier with a bad attitude towards horses, and often their owners, too, can certainly make your horse difficult to shoe, and maybe create an enduring problem for both of you.)
- When he has finished, you will settle up with him and he will get his diary out and give you another appointment in, on average, six weeks time. If, as he gets to know your horse, he wishes to shorten or lengthen this period, he will tell you.

66 Shoe to help laminitis

Laminitis is a condition that needs the immediate attention of your vet and probably your farrier if the horse is to have the best chance of surviving, let alone recovering. Foot support and specific shoeing with heart-bar shoes (see photo) can be crucial to the horse's comfort and the success of his treatment.

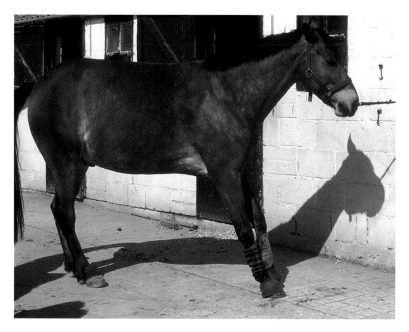

emergency nature of even a mild attack of laminitis. If you suspect an impending or existing attack, ring the vet at once for an emergency call-out. Fold up exercise bandages and tape them to your horse's feet on the frog for temporary support. Remove anything edible from your horse's surroundings. Stable him on deep, clean sawdust or shavings for inedible, cushioning support. If he has to stay out, muzzle him till the vet arrives.

- **Do not walk the horse**
- **Do not allow the administration of corticosteroids to your horse, which can make things worse**

If nothing is said about x-rays, frog supports or heart-bar shoes (see photo below), make a point of asking about them. Telephone the Laminitis Clinic (see Useful Addresses) for up-to-date advice.

How can shoeing help laminitis?

In laminitis (see also pages 128 and 129), the crescent-shaped pedal bone that gives the foot its form can become loosened or even detached from the inside of the hoof wall to which it is normally strongly bonded by means of the interlocking laminae on the bone and the wall. The bone then tilts downwards and presses down on the sensitive sole at the toe, and may even come through the sole itself. The pain is concentrated in the toe area, so the horse tends to stand on his heels to relieve it – this is a stance typical of laminitis.

For mild cases frog supports can be put on, but in others it is normally recommended that heart-bar shoes are fitted. It is essential that they are made to fit so that the point of the heart-bar coincides exactly with the toe of the bone. A marker such as a drawing pin is put in the tip of the frog, the foot is x-rayed from the side so that the drawing pin shows clearly, plus the extent of movement of the bone, and the resulting plate is studied by vet and farrier to get the shoe, and therefore the support, in exactly the right place.

What can I do?

Sadly it seems that not all veterinary surgeons, even now with the benefit of current research, accept the

67 Shoe to help navicular disease

The navicular bone is a sesamoid or 'pulley' bone deep inside the foot, behind the joint formed by the pedal (coffin) bone and the short pastern bone. The deep digital flexor tendon passes over it, the bone's job being to maintain a constant angle of attachment of the tendon to the pedal bone, reducing wear and stress on the tendon.

Understand the problem

Navicular disease is the deterioration of the navicular bone due to pressure from the deep digital flexor tendon, from general trauma and concussion. The bone can suffer extreme stresses, being squeezed up between the tendon and the coffin joint. However, there is much more hope of recovery from navicular disease now than was the case years ago; mechanical aspects of management such as trimming and shoeing are highly influential in its treatment, and homoeopathy and herbalism can offer significant support.

Symptoms and treatment of navicular disease

The pain in navicular disease is in the opposite part of the foot to laminitis: in the heel area, so either the horse places his feet down toe first and may rest a leg by placing it forwards on the toe ('pointing'), or he bends the knee and puts the leg back so the foot rests on the front wall at the toe, with the heels up. Lameness may occur in both fore feet and be hard to detect, but the horse will have a choppy gait and may trip a good deal. The feet may appear narrow and will wear most at the toes. Any drugs given will aim to improve circulation and relieve inflammation and pain.

Shoeing for navicular disease

Traditionally, egg-bar shoes (see photo above) have been used, but straight-bar shoes with more support for the back part of the frog are used more now, to increase heel and frog pressure, so encouraging expansion of, and circulation in the back part of the foot. Straight-bar shoes are also less likely to be pulled off. Wedges under the heels may be used in order to relieve tension on the tendon, and also pads (see right) to reduce concussion.

Management

The horse should be turned out on soft ground and not stabled very much, so that he can walk around and use his feet. All work involving fast trotting on hard surfaces, galloping and jumping, must stop immediately.

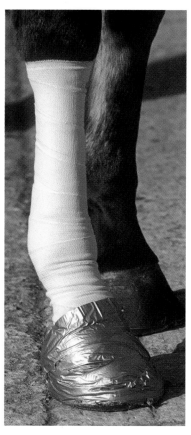

The healthy hoof

68 Investigate the barefoot option

Partly because it seems to be increasingly difficult to find a good farrier, and partly because of the increased interest in 'natural' horse care, many owners want to keep and work their horses without shoes at all (barefoot). The arguments in its favour are very convincing; in practice, however, it often does not work out. What are the pros and cons?

The advantages of going barefoot

Horseshoes undoubtedly restrict the natural expansion of the foot, and so also the blood circulation of both the foot and the lower leg. Because most shoes are of metal (mild steel being the most usual), which does not dissipate or absorb shock waves well, there is more concussion to the hoof as it impacts the ground. By definition metal is also unforgiving, so if a horse spreads, twists or breaks a shoe and it strikes his foot or a leg, the injury can be significant. Also nail holes can lead to splits that may subsequently predispose to infection.

Once they have adapted to the barefoot state, horses can cope quite happily with straightforward, steady work such as hacking out; however, they are not always so comfortable when they have to gallop and jump carrying a rider in a more demanding performance situation.

The disadvantages of going barefoot

Although the foot is encased in tough horn, the sole of the hoof is less resilient and can bruise easily; thus on hard or stony going the horse can quite readily suffer tenderness and bruising. Although the shoe is nailed to the bearing/ground surface of the horny wall of the hoof and does not actually cover the sole, it does raise the sole up and therefore clear of damaging surfaces to some extent. Even though stronger horn and thicker sole horn should be produced to help the barefoot horse cope with the harsher conditions his hooves will encounter, it will still take several months for them to adapt. Meanwhile you must be prepared to expect more cracks, chips and tenderness, and will almost certainly have to avoid abrasive, gritty surfaces, and have his hooves trimmed and balanced more frequently.

What can I do?

- Discuss fully the barefoot option with your farrier, who will still need to come and trim and balance your horse's feet at frequent intervals.
- It is important that your horse has naturally good, tough horn, but this can be helped by feeding a high quality, well balanced diet.
- An appropriate foot dressing might help (see page 105).
- Do not work on gritty, stony going for quite some time: grass, dirt tracks, prepared surfaces and perhaps smooth hard roads should be fine.
- The most important thing is to keep a close eye on your horse, and be scrupulously honest with yourself if he seems to be holding back, uncomfortable, or 'footy'. Domestic hooves are not wild ones, and going barefoot does not work for all horses and ponies by any means, whatever breed or type they may be.

69 Learn how the correct FPA maintains soundness

The intricate mechanism in the horse's leg that gives the spring to his step, and saves energy and also wear and tear on bones, horn and soft tissues, depends on well balanced feet and the correct alignment or angle of the hoof and pastern: too upright, or too sloping an angle can cause various problems that can lead to long-term lameness.

The foot/pastern axis and the horse's conformation

To a large extent the 'correct' angle depends on the horse's conformation, but there are limits either way. In general, when seen from the side on level ground, the angle formed with it by the front of the fore hoof and pastern should be about 50°, give or take a very few degrees. The hind hoof and pastern are slightly more upright.

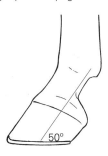

The traditional guideline is that, in a riding horse of reasonable conformation, the FPA should match the slope of the shoulder up the line of the spine of the shoulder blade. The angle of the heels should also be the same. Driving horses often have more upright shoulders than riding horses so that the collar lies more comfortably in traction.

Short toes and high heels usually result in the coronet being prominent, known as a 'broken forward' FPA (top right). This can be corrected by lowering the heels, but be aware that this shape can develop navicular disease as the horse takes less weight on the heels. Feet and pasterns that are naturally upright are more prone to concussion.

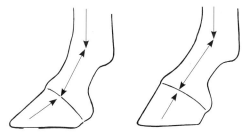

Long toes and low heels are far more common, and many Thoroughbreds have this conformation naturally. From the side, the coronet may appear to sink down, known as 'broken back' (above left), and there may even be a concave shape to the hoof wall from the side. Excessive weight is concentrated in the heel area; the pressure so created can hamper the blood circulation here and so reduce the production of horn, therefore the horse ends up with even lower, flatter heels and longer toes. The process will continue if it is not corrected.

There is considerable 'pull' or strain on the suspensory ligament and particularly the flexor tendons, and pressure on the navicular bone. The toe continues to grow forward, and the hoof wall can begin to crack due to excess pressure when the foot breaks over (turns over at the toe) in action. The horse will find it increasingly difficult to move. The white line area, between sole and wall, is pulled apart and appears widened, making it easy for white line disease to become established.

This conformation can be gradually corrected by shortening the toes from underneath the foot and maybe rolling or squaring them, and by fitting shoes with a raised heel or heel wedges to lessen the tension on the ligaments and tendons.

70 Be conscientious in daily foot care

Although a farrier's job is so specialized, there is a lot that you, the owner, can do to look after your horse's feet between visits. You should attend to his feet every day, and are in the best position to spot, and feel, any changes before they become a problem. Whether a horse has good or poor feet, they are ultimately the owner's responsibility.

Day-to-day care for a healthy hoof

Pick out and check the feet and shoes at least once a day, and always before and after work. Check for wounds or infections of the coronary band. Hooves that are constantly wet with either water or, worse, urine can become soft and weak, and attract fungal and bacterial diseases such as thrush: so check for softened horn and any bad smell or dark discharge, usually from the frog. Cleaning out the feet allows air to the underside and removes stones and other debris that can cause bruising. Check regularly horses that are out in all weathers, and also those that are stabled a great deal. All feet benefit from clean, dry standing.

The length of time between shoeings is important to your horse's comfort, soundness, agility and safety. Although an average interval is six weeks, much depends on the individual rate of growth, and the rate at which your horse wears his shoes out due to his work and the surfaces he works on. If the clenches are rising, the horn growing over the edge of the shoe, the shoe 'moving' forwards, the horn cracking or, obviously, if a shoe is loose, the shoes have probably been on for too long. Your horse's attitude and action can also change as his feet become uncomfortable.

Using the correct weight of shoe for your horse is important to his comfort and ability to work. Too light a shoe will wear out quickly and need replacing frequently, and the nail holes will damage his feet; and a shoe that is too heavy (often used for economy) will cause the horse to drop his feet with more impact, causing concussion that will in turn over-stress the soft tissues of his legs and back -- and the shoes will wear out just as quickly.

A shoe is loose if you can get the end of your hoofpick easily under the shoe at the heels and move it around; if you can move the shoe up and down and from side to side with your fingers, individual nails are obviously loose -- you will hear a tinny, clanking noise rather than

the usual firm 'clop' sound when that foot lands on a hard surface. Check these things daily; also make a point of noticing whether the clenches are rising.

Hoof oils have been part of owners' grooming kits for generations; however, now we are told that ordinary oils can interfere with the moisture balance and permeability of the foot. Other dressings have come on to the market over the past twenty years or so, but not all of them are beneficial or necessary. Brittle hooves are usually more in need of moisture than oil, and lanolin-based products are normally good for this problem. Hoof tougheners may be useful for the underfoot area, but your vet or farrier may not recommend products with iodine or formalin in them, as some can over-harden and dry the horn. Always seek professional advice on what products, if any, to use.

Hoof supplements can benefit horses with poor horn constitution, foot problems and/or those on a restricted diet. Trace elements/minerals are essential for foot health, as are the nutrients biotin (a type of Vitamin B) and the protein methionine, though the product needs to be properly balanced. Horses with good feet and enjoying an ample and well-balanced diet should not need special supplements – it is a mistake to feed them as a precaution.

Overgrown flaps of frog horn can cause problems; these usually occur down the side of the frog, trapping moist dirt underneath, which will prevent you properly cleaning the hoof, and will soften horn and attract infection. With a very sharp, strong penknife you can learn to cut off these flaps, towards the toe, without cutting the actual frog. Most farriers will show you how.

If the heels of the shoe are so close to the frog that you cannot clean in here properly, ask your farrier about tapering the shoe heels more or, if appropriate, shoeing the horse fractionally wider here.

Dental health

Maintaining teeth and health

Teeth can have as far-reaching an effect on the comfort and health of a horse, and therefore on his attitude, as they can on our own. My own dentist told me that in Victorian times and earlier, the main cause of death in humans was systemic infection due to poor or non-existent mouth hygiene – bad teeth and gum disease – and brushing teeth seems to have been unheard of.

Modern horse owners are much more appreciative of the necessity of having teeth checked regularly, although some still underestimate the importance of it. The potential problems that can be caused by the teeth or mouth being in poor condition are far-reaching; for instance under saddle, a horse that is constantly evading the bit and appears to have a bad attitude, might in fact be in pain because his teeth are sharp; and bad behaviour might be due to the distress of discomfort and pain in his mouth. Sharp or badly aligned teeth, or perhaps an ulcer in the mouth, may be the cause of persistent indigestion and repeated colic attacks, loss of condition, poor appetite and generally poor health due to poor nutrition, even if the horse is not actually thin.

Feral horses, of course, do not normally have their teeth attended to, and the argument is that because they are eating a natural diet, their teeth grow and wear as they were meant to do and they have few problems, otherwise the species would die out. In fact this is not true, and the main cause of death in feral horses, other than predation where it exists, is starvation due to dental problems. Apparently very few feral horses live to the age of fifteen. I have seen several skulls of feral equines with appalling tooth problems; one of these had razor sharp, overgrown points 4cm (2in) long on the outside of the upper cheek teeth and the inside of the lower ones, which must have been torture to live with.

Fortunately our domestic horses, although they have problems unknown to their feral cousins, do not have to put up with that sort of thing provided their owners are meticulous about regular dental care, learn a good deal about it themselves, and ask the right questions to make sure that everything that is necessary is done, and the job is not skimped.

71 Gain your horse's co-operation

What has being co-operative to do with being healthy? Well, it can be embarrassing if a horse won't co-operate with the dentist, or anyone else who comes to help him. What can we do to improve matters?

Ways to gain the horse's co-operation

We tend to feel that professionals are trained to handle 'difficult' horses, but this is not always so! Vets have one big advantage not available to the rest of us, in that if a horse is being really difficult, he can sedate it. Acepromazine (ACP) is a sedative in paste form that can be administered by the owner. However, it is not always effective in that the horse appears quieter until the procedure he dislikes is resumed, when the 'sedation' magically 'wears off' and he behaves just as badly as he did before.

As far as dentistry is concerned, the two things you want the horse to do are open his mouth, and stand still (with his head at an accessible height).

- Opening the horse's mouth is generally quite easy: stand in front of the horse's shoulder with your back to his tail, put your hand nearest him under his neck and over his face, and slip a finger of the other hand in the corner of his mouth (where the bit goes and where there are no teeth to bite you) and tickle his tongue confidently; you can actually grasp the tongue with this hand and hold it in order to keep the mouth open to take a look at the teeth.

However, persuading him to keep it open while the vet or dentist looks in is another matter, and it has to be opened very wide in order to see the back molars.

- Many horses have never been taught to stand still, nor have they been taught any basic good manners. These are basic lessons that should be instilled in the horse right from the start, at a young age. Discipline is discussed on page 109, and methods of restraint for the recalcitrant on page 123.

- Head-shy horses are not going to be cured in the five minutes before the dentist (or whoever) arrives. There are several useful and effective shiatsu techniques which, over a very few sessions, greatly help this problem (see pages 141 and 145); and natural horsemanship practitioners may concentrate on desensitizing the horse over a few sessions by gently but persistently handling the head, maybe with a stuffed glove on the end of a walking stick. However, this problem will need a great deal of input from the owner, and it will have to start several weeks before the dentist is due to come.

- Finally, quite a few horses are more co-operative with therapists and other professionals when their owner is out of sight and sound. A confident, no-nonsense, positive attitude, with a firm but not rough approach, often gets things done quickly and effectively.

Discipline

The subject of discipline has always been controversial, but certainly some ideas that are currently fashionable are excellent, and some of the techniques – for example, those of some so-called 'natural horsemanship' practitioners – work almost like magic. Some of these practitioners have rather extreme views and do not employ discipline of any kind, but use other methods of achieving co-operation that are unfortunately outside the scope of this book. Nevertheless, discipline is certainly a significant and unmistakable element of natural life in a herd of horses, feral or domestic.

It cannot be denied that many owners spoil their horses, pander to them too much, mutely accept bad manners and domineering behaviour, and are happy to go along with the act the horse is putting on (and it does happen), protecting him with the excuse 'he's not in the mood – can you come another day?' or 'he's too frightened – we'll have to leave it' or 'I don't want to upset him – let's have a coffee and we'll try later'. Some owners are actually somewhat frightened of their horse, but often his bad behaviour is simply because he is uneducated, insecure and ill-mannered – he isn't necessarily bad or vicious (although there are a few of these), but very often is looking for guidance and direction from his owner, which the owner fails to provide.

There are times when a horse is genuinely unsure or even frightened, and this may well be due to poor, even bad handling and management by a previous owner. If a horse is not educated thoroughly and correctly, he cannot be expected to know how to behave in human society. And if he has not been taught to be 'way-wise', he may in fact be very sensible to regard strange things and people with suspicion – he is a prey animal, after all.

Fortunately it is never too late for him to learn. Horses change owners, yards, friends and jobs all the time – and maybe all at the same time – and are very adaptable; they are also much cleverer than many humans think (remembering that they have equine, not human, intelligence). Therefore most horses can be greatly improved, although many ingrained behaviour patterns and attitudes will certainly stay for life.

I would advise anyone not happy with their relationship with their horse to call in professional help from someone with a calm, firm, positive attitude, who will not be impatient or rough with their horse. (Various useful addresses are given on page 150.)

72 Get a better grasp of your horse's age

The horse, like other mammals, has temporary and permanent teeth, and certain standard changes in dentition occur during his lifetime that can help us to assess his age. Even so, although this process is fairly precise in a horse under about six years of age, over that age it becomes less exact, and rather depends on the observer's education and experience.

mammals, horses' teeth erupt (rather than actually grow) throughout life. A full tooth has a crown and a root: in younger horses not much crown appears above the gum so the teeth do not appear very long, but as the crown wears down, more comes through.

- The cheek teeth are arranged in arcades (rows) of six, three premolars and three molars behind them, on each side of the upper and lower jaws. They come through at varying times from one to four years. Male horses, and very occasionally females, will also have canine teeth or tushes that start to come through at four years, the upper ones set slightly further back than the lower ones. Tiny premolars known as wolf teeth may also occur in front of the first permanent cheek teeth; there may be from one to four of them.

The temporary teeth

A foal should have a full set of temporary teeth by the age of nine months. He will have six upper and six lower front or incisor teeth, and six premolars (cheek teeth for grinding) – three each side – in the upper and lower jaws. These temporary teeth serve the young horse well as his head grows, making room for the higher number of permanent teeth.

The permanent teeth

The age of the horse when his permanent teeth come through is fairly standard, although it has been found that Thoroughbreds' teeth come through at the times stated, but others tend to erupt a little later.

- The two middle or central incisors come through at 2½ years, the lateral incisors next to them at 3½ years, and the corner incisors at 4½ years, although those in the lower jaw come through slightly later. All the permanent incisors should be in full wear, upper against lower, by the age of five years.
- Permanent incisors are yellowish in colour, larger (and stronger) than the temporary ones, and where the temporary teeth are rounded where they meet the gum, the permanent ones are squarer. Like other grazing

As the horse ages

The teeth wear best, and the horse can adopt his most natural eating pattern/jaw movement, if he eats with his head down all the time: it seems that like this, the wear on the teeth will be more even. Thus the food the horse eats, and the position of his head as he eats it, determines the type of the wear on the teeth, and the amount – and since both of these will vary from one horse to another, this is one reason why ageing an older horse is imprecise.

- The table, or biting surface of the incisors, or front teeth, which clamp together to tear off grass and leaves, is elliptical in shape in young horses, becoming round, then triangular and finally oval. A newly erupted incisor has a ring of cement on the table known as an infundibulum; this gradually wears away, and as wear continues, a brown mark of dentine appears, the 'dental star' – at first this is a line, then it becomes oval, and finally round.
- When the horse is six years old, a hook starts to form on the outer corners of the upper corner incisors; it is fully formed by seven years, and disappears by the time the horse is eight. This hook is variable in its appearance, though, and like the marks on the tables, is unreliable as a guide to age.
- When the horse reaches the age of ten years, sometimes

a little later, a brown line or shallow groove, called Galvayne's Groove, starts to show at the gum line of the upper corner incisors; as the teeth continue to wear and erupt, it will have reached the full length of the tooth at about twenty years, and it will have grown out altogether by about thirty years.

- As well as all these changes, the slope of the incisors all the time increases from being fairly straight or vertical to very forward sloping, even rather V-shaped, when seen from the side. Such teeth are also usually quite long

-- hence the expression 'long in the tooth' to indicate an old horse. This increasing slope, plus the stage of the Galvayne's Groove, is a reasonably accurate way of estimating the age of an older horse.

- The cheek teeth, too, are not without their propensity to alter, the main change being that as the teeth wear down in old horses, eventually the softer and smoother roots will become exposed. The root surfaces are naturally not so efficient at grinding up tough, fibrous food, so a softer but highly nutritious diet will be needed (see p113).

Misshapen teeth like these (left) can make it difficult for a horse to graze. A vet or equine dentist will probably want to keep an eye on them and keep them as even as possible.

Carefully move the bottom jaw from side to side (below): if the horse objects his cheek (back) teeth could well need attention.

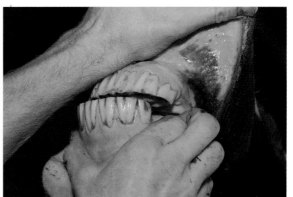

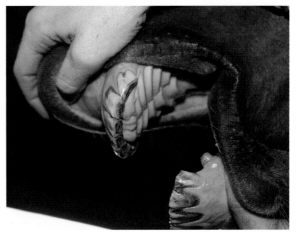

Irregularly spaced teeth like these often cause surprisingly little problem, although food may impact in the gaps, which will need cleaning out regularly.

A hard palate that is lower than the tables (biting surfaces) of the incisor teeth, as here, can make grazing and eating uncomfortable. In young horses a condition called lampas causes this effect, but usually subsides as the horse ages. This is an older horse, and this condition can be due to natural formation or infection.

73 Check out signs of discomfort in the mouth

All too often, if a horse is behaving badly under saddle it is blamed on 'attitude', although back problems may be considered; and sometimes uncharacteristic behaviour in field and stable connected with eating and drinking may go unnoticed, or be passed off as 'it's just his way', even when of recent onset. However, any change needs investigating.

Signs of discomfort in the mouth

When the horse is tacked up and working, there are certain obvious signs that indicate a problem in his mouth. The discomfort might be right inside the mouth, or it might be caused by something as simple as a noseband that is too tight. You should always be able to run a finger easily all round under your noseband, and round all the straps of your bridle. Another point to consider is that the horse's cheeks may be pinched between the bit rings or cheeks and the back teeth. A bit the wrong size, or one that the horse finds uncomfortable, can also cause problems. Sometimes the signs of discomfort are obvious, such as:

- the horse producing too much froth;
- tossing and shaking the head;
- snatching at the reins;
- resisting and leaning on the bit/poking the nose;
- the tongue coming out of the mouth;
- the horse coming behind the bit and/or going overbent (when not caused by a harsh contact from the rider).

Other signs of mouth discomfort may be less obvious, such as:

- lack of free, forward and controlled movement;
- holding the head in a peculiar posture;
- not going straight;
- bucking;
- rearing;
- napping.

Signs of discomfort that might be noticed other than when the horse is working might include:

- eating more slowly than usual;
- quidding/dropping food out of the mouth;
- holding the head strangely during eating;
- snatching/jerking movements of the head;
- playing with food or water but not eating or drinking freely;
- not eating up;
- a worried expression whilst trying to eat;
- swelling on the face (this could be an infected tooth root);
- leaning the head against the wall (sign of great pain);
- drooling saliva;
- not closing the mouth properly.

What can I do?

With the help of a sympathetic teacher, check that your horse's bridle and bit are really comfortable for him, and that your hands and contact are not too heavy, and causing him distress. The other symptoms should be investigated by a veterinary surgeon or equine dental practitioner.

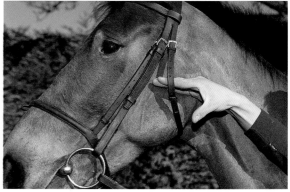

74 Adapt the feeding of a horse with dental problems

Whether a horse has an ongoing problem needing frequent attention, a temporary problem, or a permanent condition that interferes with his ability to eat, the end result will probably be that he cannot chew easily. So how can you feed him adequately without inviting colic or choke, commonly caused by poorly chewed food?

Difficulties with fibre

When a horse has dental problems he may not be able to chew such coarse feeds as hay, haylage or forage feeds containing alfalfa/lucerne and straw thoroughly enough. This can lead simply to his not eating enough. If the horse gulps food down unchewed, it can cause choke, a blockage of the gullet. If the food is swallowed it can pass through to the stomach and on down the digestive tract where it may cause an impaction, usually in the large intestine.

Certain dental problems might cause a temporarily sore mouth: for example, tooth rasping, the removal of a tooth, a broken tooth, a long tooth growing into the gap left by a missing one, sharp edges on the cheek teeth that injure the tongue and cheeks, hooks on the back teeth (sharp edges and/or points and hooks both prevent the normal chewing action of the jaws), chewing on the roots of the teeth in old horses, and uneven grinding surfaces on the cheek teeth.

What can I do?

- The horse may not be able to chew long-stranded hay and haylage properly, and a fair proportion of this may pass out undigested with the droppings. Try buying a soft type of short-chopped forage feed, such as one made entirely of grasses (no straw or alfalfa), and soak and drain it before feeding. In large enough quantities, you can replace his long forage with this, fed at ground level from a large tub cleaned out daily.
- Grazing should be possible in almost any situation. It is processed feeds that cause most problems.
- Also buy some nutritionally well balanced, very high-fibre cubes, and soak them together with sugar-beet pulp so that you have a moist, mushy feed that will satisfy the horse, be easy to eat, and provide his nutrients.
- Boiled or steamed cereals can be tried.

- Make good use of grated carrots and other roots the horse likes (he may not be able to cope with sliced carrots or quartered apples). You can make your job easier by grating them in a food processor.
- Ring the helpline at the company whose feeds you use, and get further advice and ideas from their nutritionists.
- Take the time to stand and watch your horse graze or eat in the stable to see how he is really coping.

75 Monitor natural wear patterns

Obviously an accident such as a kick that causes a broken tooth will need immediate dental treatment; but some horses have naturally deformed teeth that will always need regular care. Even those horses with a full set of perfect teeth need regular attention, simply due to the shape of the jaws, and the way they move during eating.

The way horses eat

A horse's top jaw is slightly wider than the bottom one, and the bottom jaw is set slightly back from the top one, which is why the teeth are always subject to uneven wear, even in the natural course of his life. Slight variations in jaw and tooth conformation can exacerbate or lessen the results of natural wear.

Because of the different jaw widths, the outside edges of the upper cheek teeth and the inside edges of the lower ones become overgrown and sharp. When the horse eats with his head down, the lower jaw moves

forwards slightly, enabling more even wear from front to back of the arcade than if he has to eat with his head off the ground, when the lower jaw falls back slightly. This position favours the development of hooks on the front edges of the first upper cheek teeth and the back edges of the last lower cheek teeth, and if such problems are not dealt with, even more uneven wear patterns can result.

When the permanent cheek teeth are coming through, the temporary ones may become wedged on top of them (when they are known as 'caps') and must be removed.

The incisors, too, need to meet evenly to maintain level tables. Horses

that are 'undershot' (pig-mouthed) or 'overshot' (parrot-mouthed) will have problems grazing efficiently and will eventually grow thin blades of enamel on the front and back edges of the tables. These not only interfere with grazing, but also with jaw movement and chewing.

What can I do?

- Have your horse's teeth attended to every six months by a competent equine dental practitioner (see page 115). Book the next visit each time, because the best ones are always booked up for months in advance.
- Watch your horse's demeanour and behaviour very carefully as a matter of course, so as to check for mouth discomfort.
- Standing with your back to his tail, feel with your fingertips through his cheeks up the outside edges of his upper cheek teeth in order to see how he reacts.
- Also, steadying his top jaw with one hand and with the other holding his bottom jaw, try moving it carefully and slightly from side to side, watching his reaction.
- For any other procedures it is advisable to enlist expert help for safety's sake; also, it is essential to use a gag to keep a horse's mouth safely open so that the very back teeth can be checked and treated properly if necessary.

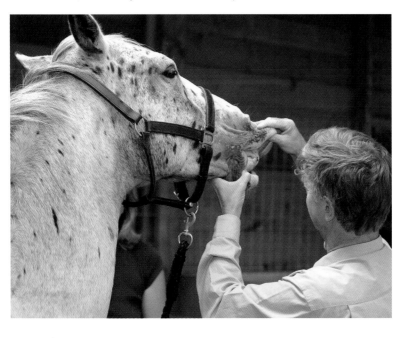

76 Check your dentist's qualification

Working on horses' teeth can range from basic jobs such as rasping sharp edges (which is not as easy as it sounds), to performing full surgical procedures such as extracting teeth. As with the craft of farriery some years ago, legal regulation is currently under way to clarify who may and may not carry out given procedures.

Qualifications and the law

Certain procedures can be performed in the UK by people whether they are trained or not. These procedures are:

- the examination of equine teeth;
- routine rasping (excluding the use of power dental tools);
- the removal of sharp enamel points and small dental overgrowths (less than 5mm high, and involving less than half of the tooth's occlusal surface) with manual rasps ('occlusal' means the tables, the biting or grinding surfaces of the teeth);
- the removal of digitally (finger) loose deciduous cheek teeth ('caps');
- the removal of calculus lying above the gum line ('calculus' is plaque or tartar).

The relatively recent qualification of Equine Dental Technician ensures that those with the letters EDT after their name, and on the members' register of the British Association of Equine Dental Technicians (BAEDT), have been adequately trained and examined in those procedures and others, both theoretically and practically. In fact the situation is currently changing to allow

EDTs to perform more advanced tasks; however it will still only be possible for veterinary surgeons to perform what are classed as 'surgical procedures', and to administer analgesics, sedatives, anti-inflammatories and antibiotics.

To get your horse's teeth attended to, you can contact either a veterinary surgeon, or an EDT, or an unqualified person who, by reputation, is known to do excellent work. If procedures other than those listed above are required, check with your veterinary practice first about the legal situation. There are many 'horse

dentists' doing a very competent job of rasping horses' teeth, removing sharp points, hooks and so on – but there are others who are injuring horses and damaging their teeth. The reputation of all professionals goes before them in the horse world, and most horse owners know of good and bad 'dentists'.

Finally, for whoever does your horse's teeth, it is only by using a gag to keep the horse's mouth sufficiently open that all the teeth, particularly those at the very back of the horse's mouth, can be properly examined and treated.

First aid skills

Be prepared

Few things cause more panic than an injured horse thrashing about, or blood all over the place and everyone running around giving conflicting advice. Four things will greatly help to ease and control the situation:

1 an unflappable temperament on your part;

2 acquiring a sound, working knowledge of first aid;

3 a well-disciplined horse who trusts you; and

4 a full, in-date first aid kit.

The treatment a horse receives immediately after his injury or suspected illness can dictate how well and how quickly he recovers. Buy a book on equine first aid that is right up to date, and really study it. Make sure it *is* up to date: look for when the book was published or *revised*, not just reprinted, which usually means that it has not actually been updated. Veterinary books soon go out of date in view of the continuing advances in equine research. Keep the book with your first-aid kit so that you can look things up when needed – note 'when', not 'if'.

Ask one of the vets or veterinary nurses at your practice what a good first aid kit should contain, and which are the best items. You should be able to buy your supplies from them, they might also recommend a good first aid book. Some practices produce their own leaflets and information booklets and also regular newsletters.

Keep your kit in a decent box or cupboard, and keep everything clean with the tops on, or wrapped up in a cool, dark place out of the reach of children or animals. However, if you lock the box, make sure people know where the key is, because if you take it home, no one can reach your supplies to help your horse in your absence. Obviously, keep your vet's 'phone number with the kit.

HOLISTIC TIP

Herbal, homoeopathic and aromatherapy remedies can be very effective in first-aid situations. You will probably get the best effects if you consult an appropriate expert such as a homoeopathic vet, a medical herbalist or a qualified aromatherapist on referral from your own vet, as they can tailor the remedy to your horse. Complementary therapies tend to treat the patient rather than the disease or disorder, but there are standard remedies to have handy for any horse. I have never known an orthodox veterinary surgeon refuse a referral to a trained and qualified complementary therapist, and most are willing to work with them.

77 Master the skill of bandaging

Bandaging is an underestimated skill. In some professional yards only the senior staff are allowed to bandage, although everyone has to learn and start somewhere. A lot of harm can be done by uneven pressure, by the bandage being too tight or too loose, or not extending far enough above and below the injury.

Tips for successful bandaging

- Bandages must be applied with even pressure, they should be put on over padding, and should not contact bony prominences such as the point of the hock or the protruding bones of the knee.
- They should be changed at intervals, as stipulated by your vet.
- It helps a bandage stay on if you extend it a good way above and below the area concerned.
- Do not, though, extend the edges of the bandage beyond the edges of the padding for fear of causing pressure or friction sores.

An injured horse may be too upset and jumpy to bandage effectively without sedation, in which case take the advice of your vet. Certain methods of restraint may, or may not work (see page 123).

1 If there is a wound, this will need a non-stick dressing over it and any medication applied, held in place by special veterinary padding.

2 This is covered by an even layer of Gamgee Tissue or cotton wool that will conform to the shape of the limb, kept in place by a stretchy conforming bandage.

3 For security, the final layer can be an elasticated, adhesive bandage (which sticks to anything, not just itself) and is very secure for the outer 'sealing' layer, as is the cohesive and popular Vetrap (which sticks lightly only to itself). You can also use an ordinary, clean exercise or stable bandage, applied comfortably and evenly. Cover the end of the bandage with adhesive tape rather than using the tapes attached to the bandage; pass it over the end of the bandage all the way round the leg and overlapping its own end.

A bandaging regime like this should stay in place, but in some cases it may be necessary to extend the adhesive bandage for half its width above the top edge on to the horse's hair. This is a last resort, and should not be done if the bandage needs changing every day. Watch the area very carefully for sores or swelling developing.

You can also apply padding and a support stable bandage below the first bandage, which will keep it from sliding down: this is particularly relevant if bandaging the knee or hock. Normally, by taking bandaging right down to the hoof you will prevent it all sliding down.

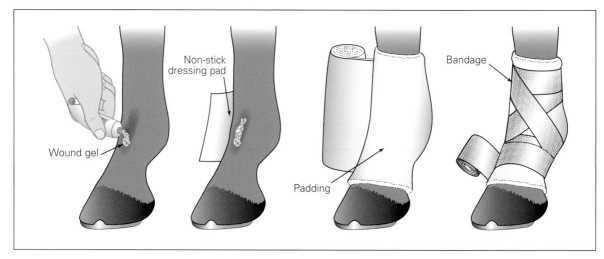

Wound gel

Non-stick dressing pad

Padding

Bandage

78 Use bandaging to help recovery when necessary

Not all injuries need bandaging, but many do, and benefit from comfortably applied, supportive and protective bandages. Smaller wounds can be protected by equine sticking plasters, although they are not always available in retail shops. Study your first aid book for detailed instructions for different bandaging techniques.

When is bandaging most likely to be necessary?

Owners are most likely to need to bandage the legs and the hooves, though special barrier boots are available for the latter, usually through your veterinary practice. Bandaging will be necessary to hold a poultice on the foot, almost always using the proprietary poultice sheet 'Animalintex' these days.

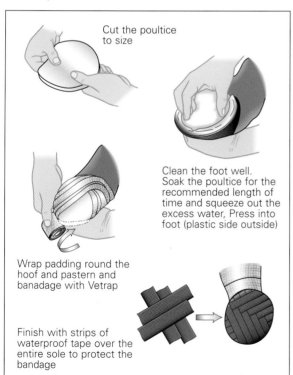

Cut the poultice to size

Clean the foot well. Soak the poultice for the recommended length of time and squeeze out the excess water, Press into foot (plastic side outside)

Wrap padding round the hoof and pastern and banadage with Vetrap

Finish with strips of waterproof tape over the entire sole to protect the bandage

In a first aid situation, bandaging is mainly used for:
- keeping dressings on wounds or other injuries;
- applying pressure to stop bleeding;
- comforting an injured and upset horse;

- protecting a wound or other injury;
- supporting strained tendons and ligaments;
- helping to keep the edges of simple wounds together;
- helping to prevent excessive proud flesh forming;
- keeping wounds clean;
- helping to control swelling;
- restricting movement, so assisting healing;
- helping to control pain; and
- preventing the horse interfering with the injury.

In cases of a leg with soft tissue strain such as might affect tendons, ligaments and other soft tissues, it is important to bandage the leg on the other side, too: for instance, the right fore if the left fore is injured. Sometimes, if a horse has injured a hind leg, he will put weight on the diagonally opposite foreleg: for instance, if he has injured his left (near) hind, he may put weight on the right (off) fore.

If the sound leg is taking a significant amount of extra weight, this extra stress could well trigger laminitis in that leg. For this reason it is advisable always to have plenty of bandaging material in your first aid kit, and also special frog supports to apply under the (clean, dry) hoof before bandaging it: this should help the horse to cope with the stress, and should also help to minimize the likelihood of laminitis. The sound leg, of course, may also become subject to stress and strain in its own soft tissues, if they have to take a lot of extra weight.

There are alternatives to bandages such as stretchy, tubular stockinette put on with a cylindrical applicator; synthetic, stretchy stockings with zip or Velcro fastenings; and special support boots similar to those often used for performance horses.

Body bandages of various sorts may be needed to protect injuries to other areas of the body, surgical or other, and your veterinary surgeon will show you how to apply these for your horse's particular injury, if necessary. Often pillowcases, tablecloths or cut-down cotton bedsheets can conveniently be used, or purpose-made body bandages.

79 Cut costs, but never compromise on nursing care

There is no doubt that veterinary dressings for injured horses can be expensive, particularly for a serious or stubborn injury that is taking its time to heal. Naturally you want to do the best for your horse -- but there are ways of saving money on dressings without compromising the efficiency of your nursing care.

There are viable alternatives

Often, buying bandaging materials for inner-layer bandaging from your chemist is cheaper than buying veterinary ones, and they can be just as good. Chemists have a wide selection of comfortable, stretchy crêpe bandages and others, so ask to see what they have, and tell them exactly what it is for. The non-giving gauze ones are not much use for horses.

Although cohesive bandages are a great help, they are not essential: they cannot often be re-used, and they are undeniably expensive. Ordinary crêpe bandages from the chemist (nice and soft and cushioning) or, if necessary, stretchy equine exercise bandages, can both be used over padding for inner-layer bandaging, whilst stable bandages can be used for the outer layer. These can all be used repeatedly, washed, disinfected, and kept clean and ready.

Most stable bandages are too short these days, and certainly for horses (as opposed to ponies) you may need to buy two sets (of four), and sew two bandages together, end to end, to make one set of bandages that are usefully long enough to cover and secure dressings. Remove the tapes and use Elastoplast adhesive tape to secure the finished bandage when it is rolled out on the leg. A cheaper alternative to Elastoplast is wide masking tape, but it has no give in it whatsoever, so do not pull it when you apply it -- just press it on.

Some stable bandages also come in non-giving materials such as velour, but as these neither stretch nor conform, they are far from ideal. Knitted cotton ones are much better, because for effective, comfortable bandaging that stays on, your bandages do need to conform. Synthetic materials are best avoided as they can make the horse's legs uncomfortably hot.

A good, economical standby instead of normal padding or branded poultices is to have a new pack of disposable babies' nappies in with your first aid kit, kept clean and sealed till needed. These can be used for various things, such as:

- when cut to size, taking medication for placing direct on to cleaned and disinfected wounds;
- again, when cut to size, as padding over veterinary dressings, such as Melolin, for wounds;
- padding under bandages in place of cotton wool or Gamgee Tissue, as they withstand repeated use better;
- carrying medication for poulticing feet, with a layer of polythene as backing.

80 Detect and identify lameness

Lameness is probably the most common problem that horse owners report, though it is not always actually called lameness. Thus the horse is described as being 'unlevel', 'uneven', 'footy', 'going short' or even 'not tracking up', 'not right' or just 'not going forward'. So what exactly is lameness?

Detecting lameness

Lameness can be defined as any change or disturbance in a horse's normal gait. If he is lame, he is incapable of a normal (for him) gait, because his instinctive way of avoiding discomfort and pain is to redistribute his weight on to another limb, or other limbs, in order to relieve the painful one, or other painful parts of the body.

- Lameness can be detected at walk and trot, but also often when the horse is just standing still, simply by the way he stands, because he will always save the affected part by relieving it of weight, and distributing that weight elsewhere. Lameness is normally graded from 0 (sound) to 10 (non-weight-bearing) in the UK. Even slight lameness can be confirmed by ultrasound once the area is detected.

- Almost any change in your horse's behaviour when he is moving, or even just standing, can indicate a potential problem; resting a foreleg forwards or backwards is a certain sign of pain, or holding a hind leg awkwardly. A change in stance can be telling: if the horse seems to stand more to one side than the other, the relieved side is the problem.

- If he starts to show anxiety when tack appears, to be unwilling to go forward, to take up transitions

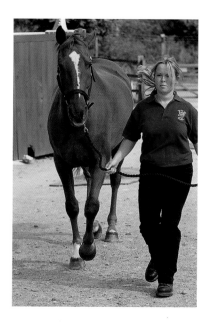

not only from one gait to another but within gaits (lengthening and shortening of stride) or to simply relax under saddle, he could have a very slight pain/lameness problem.

- More obvious signs such as resistances, playing up when ridden, and difficulty in performing simple exercises – and certainly overtly bad behaviour such as bucking, napping, running backwards, rearing, refusing to work and so on – can indicate a problem involving lameness or other discomfort or pain.

Identifying lameness

Have your horse led towards and away from you on a loose rope in walk,

then trot if he seems sound in walk. Significant lameness can be spotted at walk. Even slight lameness, though, can be spotted in trot, particularly when the horse is lunged – though he should never be lunged on a very hard surface, it is too risky.

When a horse is lame in a foreleg he will raise his head when the lame leg hits the ground to relieve it of weight, dropping it when the sound leg hits the ground. When a horse is lame in a hind leg the hip and hock of the lame leg will remain higher than those of the sound leg or rise when the lame leg hits the ground. If a horse is lame in both fore- or hind legs, the stride will be pottery and shortened, and the head will be held up and stiffly throughout.

121

81 Accustom the horse to handling and treatment

Horses are naturally suspicious of anything potentially uncomfortable or painful, but there is nothing more frustrating or annoying than a horse who will not allow himself to be handled for examination or treatment. It is much more difficult to help a recalcitrant horse than one who submits with confidence to handling.

Understanding his viewpoint

Animals are often more difficult to handle than children. You can explain to a child what is happening (which may or may not help!), but you cannot do this with an animal – and horses are big, very strong animals that tend to panic easily. I find that veterinary surgeons are much more likely to sedate a horse today, or request that he is brought into the practice for restraint in stocks, than was the case years ago. This is maybe because horses generally are not so well behaved or disciplined as perhaps they were in the past, and also because health and safety requirements are much more prominent in all aspects of life. Many vets are less inclined to take risks -- and why should they, when the owner has failed to train or accustom the horse to handling and treatment?

The horse may well view his body as his private property and only submit to pleasant or at least non-threatening handling. When things start to get unpleasant or even slightly painful, he may draw the line and object in no uncertain terms.

What can I do?

Whoever takes charge of this project needs to adopt a very firm, positive, determined and calm attitude.
- A technique that is usually reliable is for one person to hold the horse in a bridle or nose chain whilst someone else gradually, maybe over days or weeks, handles him all over, including the head and 'private parts', holds up a leg, strokes the ears and so on, talking calmly but authoritatively all the time, and praising with words and treats when the horse submits to being handled. Firmly but gently persist with 'difficult' areas, very gradually breaking down the horse's resistance, using praise and rewards – giving him a titbit or by stroking him.
- A method that works well is to have a stuffed glove on the end of a walking stick and use it to desensitize the horse by touching and stroking him (not tickling or poking) from a safe distance. Low-key, persistent insistence is what is needed. Many people also swear by clicker training to accustom and train horses.
- The horse should also understand 'no' as a signal of what is not wanted, both on the ground and under saddle. This is natural herd logic and practice, and horses certainly understand it.
- The handler also needs to understand when a horse is being 'precious' or is genuinely worried.

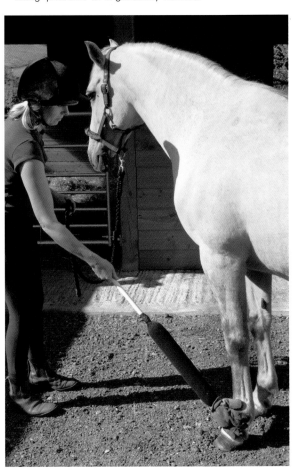

82 Learn methods of restraint

There may be times when ordinary handling and accustoming/desensitizing a horse to worrying procedures are not enough on their own. At such times, physical or chemical restraint is needed for essential veterinary treatments, or even to carry out some straightforward but important management practice for the horse's well being.

Techniques to restrain horses

- The headcollar leadrope can be passed over the nose and held beneath the jaw to apply pressure on the nose; if the elbow of the same arm is pressed into the horse's neck, this often helps to discourage him from leaning on the handler.

- Hold up and carefully twist a fold of skin on the neck in front of the shoulder: this steadies many horses, as does holding up a leg when legs are being treated. If treating a foreleg, hold up the opposite one; if treating a hind leg, hold up the foreleg on the same side.

- The upper lip has many acupressure points which, when activated, trigger the release of the body's painkillers and tranquillizers, endorphins and encephalins, a process that takes a few minutes. This can be done by squeezing the upper lip with your fingers, but it may be more practical to use a humane twitch. This firmly clamps on to the upper lip, and can be fastened to the headcollar, leaving the hands free.

- A more traditional twitch is a wooden stick with a cord loop through the end; the handler passes a hand through the loop, grasps the horse's upper lip and puts the loop round it, twisting it carefully so as not to cut the lips, until a firm but not tight pressure is achieved. Be aware that this technique does not work for all horses, and is a short-term remedy, anyway.

- After 20 minutes maximum it should be removed and the top lip rubbed to restore circulation, and examined for any abrasions from the loop. As the twitch is removed, some horses throw their heads about and become very restive or even violent.

- Dosing the horse with acepromazine (ACP) before treatment may make him drowsy, but as soon as something is tried that he finds objectionable, such as bathing a wound, he will override the effects of the drug; it is therefore not much use as a restraint.

- For difficult horses, chemical sedation (by injection) is very effective. It can only be applied by a veterinary surgeon, but it is far better to go to this trouble and expense than to risk injury to horse and handlers and possibly teach the horse that he can overcome methods of restraint – and once a difficult horse knows this, it can make handling him in the future ineffective and dangerous. This attitude will not be popular with some, but sometimes 'needs must' for the horse's welfare and health and for the safety of all concerned.

Chronic health problems

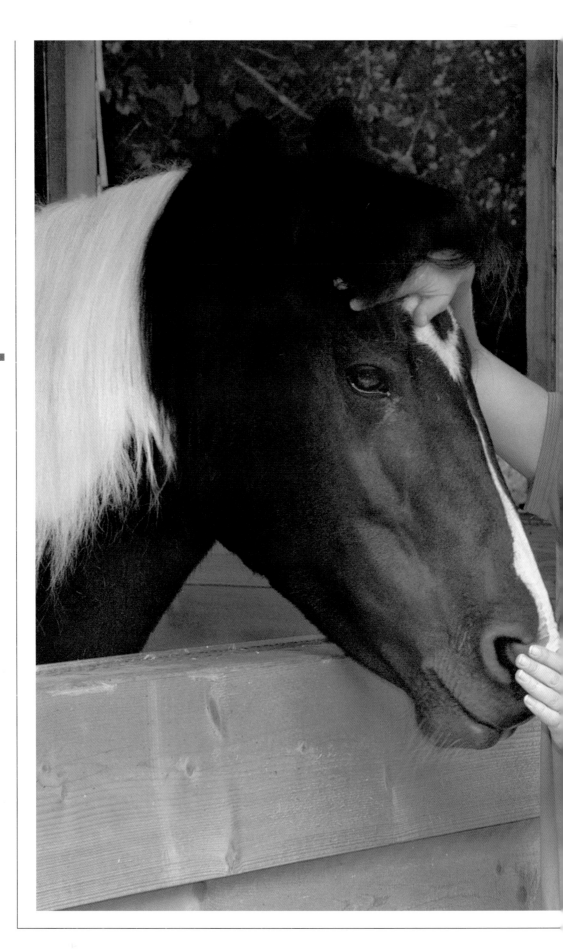

Managing chronic health problems

The expression 'as strong as a horse' gives the accurate impression that horses and strength are synonymous. Horses have been used by man for their strength for thousands of years, but strong though they are, they are not indestructible and are subject to illness and injury like any other living creature. Sometimes their disorders take hold, become chronic (long-lasting), and just have to be managed and lived with.

Sometimes these sorts of problem are the result of a preceding disease or injury; for instance, broken wind, heaves or recurrent airway obstruction (RAO) (formerly known as chronic obstructive pulmonary disease (COPD)) can follow a respiratory disease such as influenza or strangles; and chronic ligament damage can result from hard work and repeated stress and injury earlier in life. Laminitis is another condition to which a horse can become prone after once suffering an attack.

In fact chronic health problems can often be successfully managed, sometimes just by good horse care, and sometimes with veterinary help, appropriate nutrition and complementary therapies. Only a human generation ago a horse with RAO was considered beyond veterinary help, and in the same way much more recently was a horse with navicular disease. Now, both those conditions and others can often be successfully managed, to the extent that sufferers can lead relatively active and comfortable lives.

The important point is that owners – and livery yard proprietors – must be prepared to accommodate a horse's problem, and this can be done quite easily, given a caring and willing attitude. They need to provide the required facilities, and to follow an appropriate management and care regime so the horse has what he needs to cope with his problem, to remain happy and comfortable, and if at all possible, doing a useful job of work that he enjoys and which is well within his capabilities.

This latter aspect goes an amazingly long way towards keeping a horse young in body and spirit. And if he cannot work, a job as a cared-for companion – and his humans must make sure he knows that his services are needed and valued – can be just as good. Or perhaps he can be led out from another horse on hacks, or at least taken for walks out in hand by his owner.

As in most things, human attitude is everything.

83 Operate a clean air régime

Recurrent airway obstruction (RAO) is a surprisingly common disorder. It is often called 'broken wind' (or 'heaves' in the US) and emphysema; its former scientific name was chronic obstructive pulmonary disease. Horses with RAO are a sad sight, sometimes struggling for breath even when standing still -- but help is readily available.

What is RAO?

This condition is an allergic reaction to fungal spores found on organic material such as forage and bedding; it can also be triggered by general dust in the environment. At certain times of year it can be triggered by pollen, when it is known as summer pasture associated obstructive pulmonary disease (SPAOPD). Ammonia given off by urine in the bedding also damages the lining of the airways and adds to the situation.

This hypersensitivity to these irritants can be caused by inadequate convalescence after a respiratory disease: at least a month in a fresh air environment (and only walking) is needed for the airway linings to heal and recover their ability to clear the airways. They do this by means of tiny projections called cilia that carry debris away up the airways and trachea.

When horses and ponies become sensitive to the irritants involved, their immune systems over-react. Special cells called mast cells produce too much histamine and other substances, which cause spasm and narrowing of the muscles of the airways. Excess mucus is produced, and inflammation (with its swelling and soreness) occurs. The result of all these reactions is a greatly reduced airspace in the lungs and airways, and irritation of the airways. The damaged airway lining thickens and loses some of its ability to clear the airways.

Horses with RAO often stand with their nostrils flaring and the head held out and down to maintain a straight, unobstructed air passage along the nostrils and windpipe. Their respiration and heart rates are normally increased even without exercise, as the body demands, and the heart tries to supply, oxygen; the heart may enlarge with the stress of its efforts to pump more blood to supply more oxygen to the body. These horses usually develop a chronic, persistent cough, which is also productive (bringing up mucus).

The more severe cases make a quite forceful effort to breathe out, a process that is normally a natural recoil as the respiratory muscles relax after inhaling. This action develops the abdominal muscles and may result in a line known as the 'heaves line' along the bottom border of the ribcage between the chest and the belly. Depending on the severity of the case, a horse's ability to work will be reduced, and weight loss and a general unthrifty appearance will develop.

What can I do?

- Your veterinary surgeon can assess the extent of the problem by examining the horse's appearance and reaction to exercise, by endoscopic examination of the airways, and by washes to obtain material from the upper airways, which can then be examined under a microscope.
- He or she can prescribe various drugs that aim to reduce the production of mucus and histamine, reduce inflammation, relax the muscles of the airways, and generally make the horse feel much better; however, the effects will not be felt fully unless the horse is put on a clean air regime.
- Briefly, the horse should have dust-free feed and bedding, be fed from the ground, be out as much as is practicable, and be kept in a generally clean environment. Use a damp cloth to remove dust from all surfaces (see below). Old banks in stables, dusty rafters and urine-soaked bedding all invite trouble. Exercise should be at the vet's discretion; however, many affected but correctly managed and treated horses can lead very active lives.

84 Practise management for sweet itch

One of the most distressing equine conditions is sweet itch. It is an allergic reaction to the saliva of biting culicoides midges, resulting in extreme itching and irritation, inflammation, and the irresistible urge to rub on anything available. This results in raw and bleeding areas of skin that attract more insects and can become infected.

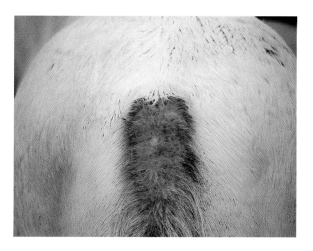

Can it be cured?

Research is currently under way to develop a vaccine against this allergy, but at present there is no cure as such. There are various ointments and lotions aimed at relieving the itching and sores, but with varying success. The areas mostly affected are the crest of the neck and the root of the tail, although the midges may bite anywhere. The condition can start as early as February in a mild year: basically, as soon as the midges start flying, sweet itch can start, and continue until late autumn or early winter, depending on the weather.

Preventive management is the answer

- Start very early in the year so that sweet itch does not develop. The midges are most active just before and after dawn and dusk, which can make turning out and bringing in susceptible animals problematic.
- The major and most highly effective weapon against sweet itch is to use a sheet that prevents the midges reaching the horse's skin to bite. The Boett Blanket (see Useful Addresses) is proving a godsend to afflicted equines and also their owners. It is a special weave of lightweight mesh that covers the horse from ears to tail and under the belly. There are other anti-midge sheets that some also find effective.
- Insect repellents, particularly those containing a high proportion of DEET, help to keep the midges away, so both in the stable and out, normal insect-repelling techniques should be employed, on the horse and the stable. (Insecticides kill insects but do not repel them, whereas repellents aim to stop them landing in the first place.)
- Affected animals should be indoors at the worst times if not wearing a sheet, although midge bites can occur at any time.
- Muslin and other screens can be placed over stable openings to prevent the midges from entering, and if the horse does become affected, consult your veterinary surgeon as to the best product to use to ease his discomfort. The use of corticosteroids is helpful in allaying inflammation, but it carries the significant risk of triggering laminitis.

85 Prevent laminitis occurring

Laminitis is one of the most painful diseases that can afflict a horse or pony, and the general conception that only fat ponies and cobs are susceptible is quite wrong. Although obesity, or being even slightly overweight, is certainly a common cause, there are others, and laminitis is one of the most common reasons for equines being crippled for life, or having to be put down.

What causes laminitis?

There are several trigger factors for laminitis, but the main cause is being overweight, and certainly obesity: see Condition Scoring (page 58) and Over-feeding (page 60) so you can be sure you know the parameters for a healthy condition for your horse. The administration of corticosteroids (a type of anti-inflammatory drug) is known to trigger laminitis, as can any other medication that disturbs the blood or the chemical balance of the gut, such as antibiotics. Other causes include:

• disorders that cause toxaemia ('blood poisoning');
• delayed cleansing after foaling;
• coming into season, in some cases;
• pneumonia;

• abscesses;
• worming and vaccinations: all procedures and administrations of this nature should be handled on veterinary advice;
• anything poisonous or toxic that the horse eats;
• anything physically or emotionally stressful, such as travelling, a change of yard, the loss of a friend, and sometimes sudden changes in weather, particularly to cold temperatures;
• hormonal disorders;
• animals with Cushing's disease frequently contract associated laminitis;
• concussion.

Comfortable feet are essential to horses, and if one foot or leg is uncomfortable, or the horse is actually lame, he will take more weight on another leg and foot, usually its opposite partner. This creates excess weight-bearing and mechanical stress on that leg and foot, which may then develop laminitis (see page 100 for more information on this).

Adapt your management

Bear in mind all the above causes, and even if your horse has not, to your knowledge, had laminitis, be aware of the circumstances that can cause it. In particular, watch what your horse eats, keep stress to a minimum, and keep his weight down to a healthy level.

86 Take immediate action in cases of laminitis

If your horse does go down with laminitis, the best way to control its effects quickly is to take action immediately to ameliorate the condition. Do not wait to see if the horse gets better on his own, because the longer this disease is left, the more likely that it will progress, and that permanent damage will be caused. It is therefore essential to be constantly on the watch for symptomatic behaviour.

The symptoms of laminitis

- Be very sensitive to your horse's facial expressions and general demeanour, as these will tell you when he is feeling unwell or in pain, as opposed to just sleepy.
- General signs of pain are patchy sweating, cold sweats, groaning in bad cases, and shifting the weight off the feet.
- Specific symptoms of laminitis are the horse standing on his heels (front or back), holding his feet up so as to take the pressure off the sole, lying down and not wanting to get up, finding it difficult to walk on rough ground or at all, and a stronger pulse than is normal in the digital arteries just above the fetlock.

What can I do?

- Laminitis is always an emergency, so you shouldn't hesitate to ring your vet for a visit immediately.
- If the animal is in a field, try to transport him to his stable, as walking can cause great damage to the internal structure of the foot. He must be bedded on a clean shavings bed at least 1ft/30cm deep, with no food (including hay) available, but plenty of clean water, until the vet arrives.

- If there is no stable available, muzzle him so that he can drink but not eat, pending further veterinary advice. Stay with him to keep him still. you should let him lie down.
- Read page 100, which gives details of frog supports. Support certainly both feet of a pair but maybe also all four feet to guard against weight-bearing laminitis occurring in the unaffected feet (see previous page).
- In the UK we are fortunate to have the Laminitis Clinic (see Useful Addresses), which will give you and your vet the latest advice over the 'phone. You can play a crucial part in your horse or pony's recovery by following veterinary instructions to the letter. Drug treatment will probably involve giving non-steroidal anti-inflammatory drugs (NSAIDs) such as phenylbutazone. Strict dieting but not starvation will be required: the horse needs a restricted diet, but with specific nutrients for hoof health and good body condition.
- There are branded feeds that are recommended for equines prone to laminitis, so ring feed companies to find out what they produce. Your vet may advise you to avoid any feed containing cereals (starch), and also to avoid long periods at grass. Only in mid-winter is grass safe to feed ad lib to such animals.

87 Help a horse to cope with box rest

The words 'box rest' usually send a chill down the spine of caring horse owners, especially if it is going to be for weeks' or even months' duration. We all know that horses need exercise, they want to be with their friends, they need to be on the move (although many are confined far too much these days). Just how do you cope?

Is box rest really necessary?

If a veterinary surgeon says that box rest is necessary, it is necessary, and it means exactly what it says: the horse indoors and nowhere else for however long the vet advises.

What can I do?

Horses actually adapt surprisingly well to box rest: very few go out of their minds, and you can do a great deal to help. Make sure that:

- the horse can always see and, if possible, touch another horse;
- he is stabled where he can see what's going on;
- he always has plenty of clean water and, depending on veterinary advice regarding diet, forage to eat.

Those are the three main basics to implement, but otherwise there are various ways you can keep him amused; these include:

- horse toys, such as footballs on the floor, or suspended on a rope or in a haynet;
- feed balls, placed on a spot where there is no bedding, and which release horse nuts when the horse rolls them around;
- frequent visits to the horse to talk to him, adjust his rugs, skip out bedding and pick out feet (most important), change water (not just fill it up), fill hay tubs and so on. Bring his friend or friends to talk to him over the door, too, if they cannot be stabled next to each other;
- depending on what is wrong with the horse, a thorough grooming every day, including refreshing sponging, to stimulate and clean his coat and skin. Wisping, hand rubbing, gentle massage and shiatsu can all help (see pages 141, 144–5).

Some people advocate a radio, but I would suggest that nearly all horses dislike a radio playing in the stable area, and show clear signs that they are irritated by the noise. Very short periods of soothing music may be accepted, but watch the horse clearly for signs of tension: head nodding (not necessarily in time to the music!), swaying and weaving, nostrils drawn up and back, or walking round and round the box (the last thing you want in cases of lameness) – are all clear signs of distress.

The main concern should be to make the horse feel that he is still involved and important.

88 Consider the pros and cons of phenylbutazone

Phenylbutazone is probably one of the cheapest and most generally used painkillers for horses. It is very effective for conditions such as gastro-intestinal pain, chronic laminitis, arthritic conditions and injured soft tissues -- but it does have disadvantages, and you have to balance your horse's need against these.

How does it work?

Phenylbutazone (commonly known as 'bute') is an NSAID, that is, a non-steroidal anti-inflammatory drug. It eases pain and reduces inflammation by blocking the production of hormones called prostaglandins, involved in the body's inflammatory response to injury. It can be given intravenously (by injection into a vein) or orally, into the mouth, in a paste, or by means of powder or tablets in food.

After an injection, it takes about 30 minutes for 'bute to start blocking the production of prostaglandins and easing the situation. It takes two or three hours for orally administered 'bute to start to be absorbed from the gut, so there is no significant relief for three to five hours, while the liver breaks down prostaglandins already in circulation. Phenylbutazone relieves pain, therefore, for about 12 to 24 hours, depending on the severity of the condition. After this time, the prostaglandins, the inflammation and the pain return. It is, therefore, no use administering it two or three times a week, as is sometimes done.

Care must be taken not to let a horse on 'bute become dehydrated because of the toxicity caused, which can be fatal.

What are the disadvantages?

The main disadvantages of any long-term use of 'bute, as it is usually known, are damage to the gastro-intestinal tract (because of the lack of its protective prostaglandins), and to the kidneys and liver. Its bitter taste will put off some horses from taking it, although it can be disguised by keeping it in the freezer or a very cold refrigerator and giving it when still cold.

What are the alternatives?

- Arnica and rhus tox are two homoeopathic remedies prescribed for pain, depending on the exact type of the problem and the cause of the pain.
- There are several herbal remedies used to ease inflammation and pain, and fenugreek may be helpful for gut damage.
- It is advised that a homoeopathic veterinary surgeon and a medical herbalist should be consulted to help with the long-term therapy and management of horses in chronic pain.

89 Understand the causes of colic

Colic is common in horses, partly due to the imperfect design of their digestive systems. It is extremely painful for the horse, and can result in having to put him down. It is another of those conditions that should always be treated as an emergency situation needing immediate veterinary attention.

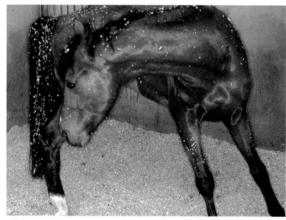

SYMPTOMS OF COLIC

Most people are familiar with the signs of colic; these include:

- the horse kicking and biting at, and looking round at his belly;
- getting up and down;
- patchy sweating;
- groaning and thrashing about, looking ill and very uncomfortable;
- sitting on the manger or wedging himself into a corner;
- high pulse and respiration (indicating pain);
- pawing, grinding the teeth, lying on the back and writhing;
- absence of, or excessive, gut sounds, and altered droppings;
- performing the flehmen response (curling the upper lip);
- stretching out the hind legs as if to stale;
- restlessness and a tight belly (flatulent or gas colic).

What causes colic?

Sometimes colic occurs for no apparent reason, and none that is ever discovered. Certainly the structure of the large intestine does not help the horse -- not least at a point called the pelvic flexure, which narrows greatly and can become blocked. Colic literally means abdominal pain, and can have other causes than digestive ones; however, here we consider the latter:

- Internal parasites (worms) can cause colic by damaging the gut lining and function. Some can block the intestines, and some accumulate in arteries and cut off the blood supply to the gut, causing tissue death.
- Feeding a low quality diet with large amounts of indigestible fibre (lignin) can cause colic – very poor, fibrous grass, for instance, and straw. Horses on straw beds with an insufficient forage supply will eat their beds and may get colic.
- Lack of water or refusal to drink can dehydrate the horse, resulting in colic. This may occur in over-heated horses, either from work or from simply standing in hot conditions such as a paddock without shelter, or a stifling, muggy trailer, horsebox or stable on a hot day.
- High-concentrate/low-fibre diets can cause colic because fibre is needed to stimulate gut movement. Too much starch can spill over into the large intestine, which is not best equipped to digest it, disturbing the intestinal micro-organisms. In horses on such diets, gastric ulcers can also cause colic-type pain and symptoms.
- Poor quality feed, feed that is 'off', and poisonous plants may also be implicated. Horses that are debilitated may not have a well functioning digestive system: if such horses are suddenly 'pumped' with food and other

HOLISTIC TIP

Complementary therapies such as homoeopathy, herbalism, aromatherapy, acupuncture and flower remedies can all significantly help a horse, not only whilst he is suffering an attack of colic, but also during his recovery. Moreover, they can help in his management if he is prone to colic.

medications, colic may occur; so the process should be gradual.

- Some drugs and medications, including wormers and antibiotics, can trigger colic, as can poor teeth (because food will not be adequately chewed), intestinal infections, working hard soon after feeding, the ingestion of sandy soil when grazing, and other causes.

Why does colic recur?

Usually because the cause has not been detected and removed – although it is sometimes very difficult to find the cause if it is not obvious. Accurate diagnosis is crucial, and at least in the UK, only veterinary surgeons will be able to make such diagnoses. Also,

after medication for colic (painkillers and other drugs) there may be digestive disturbance, which in itself causes colic to recur.

What can I do?

It is important to realize that even some of the best kept horses can go down with colic; it is not always someone's fault. However, there are some aspects of management that you should observe in order to minimize the chances of colic:

- Make sure your management is impeccable.
- Be very familiar with the signs of colic so you spot it at once.
- Keep a good balance between fibre and concentrates (if the latter are used) and make sure all feed is good quality.
- Keep your horse's teeth in good order.
- Avoid stress as far as possible.
- Worm in accordance with your vet's instructions.
- Make changes in diet very gradually, over at least two weeks or more.
- Try not to graze on sandy soils.

If your horse does go down with colic...

- Ring your vet immediately.
- Remove all food, and muzzle the horse if he is on straw bedding. Ask for instructions over the phone whilst waiting for the vet to arrive. For instance, some vets believe in gently walking the horse around to keep the gut moving, but some don't.
- If the horse gets violent, get out of his stable: there is nothing you can do and there's no point in both of you being out of action. Talk to him soothingly over the door in such a situation.

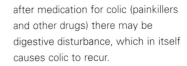

90 Manage allergies effectively

Allergies can be most frustrating to deal with, and they are often confusing to owners because they are not caused by 'germs' like ordinary infections, but often by an immune system fault, it is believed. Many allergies can be dealt with by specific treatment and effective individual management -- but some are still mysteries.

What causes allergies?

Sweet itch and 'broken wind' or RAO appear to be the most common equine allergies. Fortunately, both these conditions can now be managed reasonably well and are covered in this book. Other allergies include photosensitivity and urticaria. What causes them is an extremely complex question that cannot yet be satisfactorily answered in full. Some allergies are genetic and run in families, apparently often those containing much inbreeding – but not always. The individuals from such families have a 'weakness' or propensity to succumb to certain allergies but, as in humans and other animals, sometimes only one animal or one person in a family is afflicted.

The immune system's workings are normally unnoticeable to us. When alien substances and pathogens (germs) invade the body – which they can do through any opening, not only the normal orifices (nostrils, mouth etc), but also wounds or weakened skin -- the proteins in them (antigens) are recognized by specialized cells in the immune system; alerted to this invasion, the immune system makes other proteins called antibodies that are specifically designed to fight off that particular invader. A chain of biochemical reactions takes place, and the body's normal response to invasion and injury – inflammation – occurs within minutes.

Usually the invaders are overcome without our ever knowing about it. These events can occur daily, because these usually microscopic intruders are all around us. Sometimes, though, for unknown reasons, the immune system over-reacts to a problem (like a temperamental horse), and all the signs of an allergic response arise.

It must be said that allergies seem to be far more prevalent today than they were decades ago – it could be that increasing pollution, plus the breakdown of the world's ozone shield, are the prime culprits. Genetic change can be caused by light rays, because these can alter the very atomic structure of the nuclei of living cells, causing altered functioning. Synthetic substances of very many kinds -- not least those we can regard as pollutants – then become prevalent in all environments and affect the natural functioning of living things, including our immune systems.

There is almost nowhere in England, for instance, that is free from some kind of pollution.

Furthermore it is not only ourselves and our animals that are affected, not to mention wildlife both animal and vegetable: so are the microscopic organisms that can cause illness and allergic responses in us. They, too, have lives, and respond to their environment. They succumb or resist, like us, and they adapt or perish, like us – and this invisible war, of which only the results are seen, goes on and on.

What can I do?

- In fact the prognosis is not all bad, but in order to cope with a horse with an allergy it is normally necessary to change our management of him, sometimes very significantly and for the rest of his life. We, too, adapt to this new way of coping, and it becomes a habit and normal routine before long.

- Veterinary science has a lot to offer us, and fortunately research continues on many allergies, from sweet itch and RAO to allergies to feed, to environmental factors, and into immune system functioning and disorders.

- Coping with an allergic condition is usually a multi-pronged approach. Your orthodox veterinary practice should be able to help, depending on the condition, in the way of knowing the protocol involved in finding out what your horse is allergic to. Management advice can be given and, again, complementary therapies are often extremely effective in dealing with allergies.

- Help could come from something as basic as eliminating as much stress as possible from your horse's life. Stress alters the body's biochemistry and is debilitating in itself, which certainly does not help the immune system to function optimally. Different feeding, turnout hours, clothing, bedding, environment and treatments can all help on a management level.

- One thing is certain: it is the owner who is the key to improving an allergic condition in his or her horse, not only by his or her own actions, but also through instructions to the horse's other carers or, when necessary, finding other accommodation for him.

91 Ease the discomfort of the arthritic horse

Arthritis in its various forms does not affect only older animals. There are various forms of this bone and joint disease, but the condition is always disabling, painful and, therefore, debilitating. However, it can be managed so that horses can be made reasonably comfortable, and continue at a less demanding level of work

What is arthritis?

Osteoarthritis or degenerative joint disease (DJD) is a group of degenerative joint diseases. It is seen most commonly in the conditions known as ringbone and bone spavin, although it can affect almost any joint. The cartilage covering the ends of bones, and which makes movement smooth and painless, deteriorates to the extent that the bones are wearing against each other (which is extremely painful). The membrane in the joint that secretes the sticky, lubricating fluid called synovia is damaged, as are associated ligaments, so the horse finds movement difficult and painful.

Because he does not use the limb normally, the muscles atrophy ('shrink'), and the limb or limbs, and indeed the whole horse, becomes weaker and weaker. The pain alone is very debilitating. There is inflammation in and around the joint, and usually hard swellings due to the body producing new bone to make up for the wear and tear on the joints -- although these bony protrusions often make matters worse.

Young horses afflicted with abnormalities of the epiphyses or growth plates at the ends of the long leg bones often develop limb deformities or crooked legs, which therefore experience uneven stresses and weight bearing. These conditions often result in DJD, and older horses that have worked hard may also develop it, even if they have the best conformation.

Can arthritis be avoided?

Probably in a very well conformed horse who did little work and experienced little stress on his limbs and body, arthritis would be unusual – but of course, that would be an unusual situation. Human athletes who have had the best of training and nutrition are still prone to osteoarthritis later in life, just from wear and tear. Humans, dogs and horses seem particularly prone to the condition.

Working horses on uneven surfaces, hard surfaces regularly and rough ground, all result in concussion and uneven weight-bearing, which can favour the development of DJD.

What can I do?

- Treatment usually consists of anti-inflammatories and pain relief, phenylbutazone being probably the most practical drug to use because it is effective and economical. However, it does nothing to repair the degenerating cartilage. Steroidal drugs are not normally used in horses for relief of the symptoms of DJD because of the large doses needed and the negative side effects, although they may be commonly used in dogs with advanced DJD.
- Injections into the joint of hyaluronate or polysulphated glycosaminoglycan can help if the condition is not advanced, as can feeding a dietary supplement containing glycosaminoglycans and chondroitin sulphates. These substances can assist in the regeneration of cartilage, because a common factor in the various forms of DJD is the loss of glycoproteins (also called mucopolysaccharides) from the cartilage.
- Vitamin C is also helpful because not only is it a powerful anti-oxidant (anti-oxidants help to combat diseases

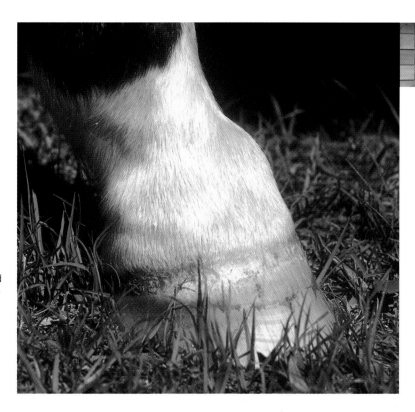

of ageing), but it can encourage the growth of cartilage.
- High protein diets should be avoided, and it is essential that vitamins and minerals should be properly balanced; therefore, consult a nutritionist to help you devise the best diet for your horse's situation.
- Herbal supplements containing saponins (these are plant versions of glycosides) are also often found to be helpful in general, whilst specific homoeopathic remedies, according to individual assessment by a homoeopath or homoeopathic vet, are very effective.
- Other complementary therapies such as acupuncture/acupressure/shiatsu and magnetic therapy can help, too.
- It is well worth explaining matters to your farrier, who may discuss with you concussion-absorbing pads under the shoes, and synthetic shoes that may reduce concussion.
- Exercise should be continued gently under veterinary instructions. Horses with DJD need to be gently on the

move most of the time, so the type of livery yard which severely restricts turnout, as do many these days, is of no benefit to arthritis sufferers especially.
- Horses with DJD should work only lightly on hard surfaces. Roadwork should be limited to walking, and any kind of fast or concussive work should certainly be avoided.
- The general management of horses with arthritis involves keeping them comfortably warm and dry, but not over-cosseted. Distress from poor management seems to exacerbate the condition. It is better to turn them out on well drained pasture wearing a decent turnout rug in winter than to keep them in and static, because they do need to move.
- A high standard of care, plus the help of your vet, complementary therapists and nutritionist, can give an arthritic horse several, indeed many, years of comfortable living and a job to do.

92 Treat tendon and ligament injuries promptly

Ligaments, tendons and muscles are termed 'soft tissues', as opposed to bony tissue, that is. Ligaments keep the bones of the skeleton in place, within limits, and the tendons, stemming from muscles, assist in movement. Injury to tendons and ligaments can be painful and enduring, and can permanently reduce a horse's level of performance.

How are ligaments and tendons injured?

The horse's muscles are his power house, which, along with nervous control and fuel delivered to and stored in them, create movement of every sort. Muscle tissue is heavy – it contains a lot of fluid, including blood -- 'elastic', and easily injured, but it also heals well if treated correctly.

Tendons and ligaments are a different story. They are fibrous in nature and only very slightly elastic. They are well supplied with nerves, which makes them sensitive, but they have a poor blood supply. Because blood is responsible for nourishing and maintaining tissue (as almost every other tissue in the body), lack of it means that injuries to tendons and ligaments have a poorer 'service' and heal more slowly.

Ligaments mainly attach bone to bone or cartilage to bone, whereas tendons attach muscle to bone. In a

simple arrangement, a muscle is attached by tendon tissue to one bone at one end (its 'origin'), and to another bone at the other end (its 'insertion'). When the muscle contracts or shortens, this creates a pull on the tendon, which causes the bone on which it is inserted to move at the joint between them.

Injuries to tendons and ligaments occur mainly due to stress, strain and sprain. Stress is the application of force, which can be a good thing if modified, as during a fitness programme, for instance. Too much can put strain on the tissues, usually the muscles, which are over-stretched when strained and possibly torn. A strained tendon or ligament is one that has been over-stretched, and a sprain is the wrenching or twisting of a joint, its over-extension or over-flexion, which will partially rupture the ligaments, and which stretches and tears the structures including blood vessels, nerves, tendons and associated muscles. A sprain, therefore, is more serious than a strain.

Such injuries can occur in the field, but most injuries, and usually the most serious ones, occur during athletic work, particularly galloping and jumping when horses are working at or near their peak ability and the tissues reach the limits of the force they can bear.

Healing and treatment

- The fibres of the tendons and ligaments have a structure that is destroyed when it is torn during injury. Tendon and ligament injuries are painful because they are supplied with nerves that register the pain. Fluid escapes from tissues and from torn, neighbouring blood and lymph vessels, causing heat and swelling. Pain, heat and swelling, of course, together mean inflammation.

- Inflammation continues for at least 48 hours in an attempt to bring nutrients and oxygen to the injury, and to clear away toxins and debris (damaged tissue cells). Because inflammation can be excessive, causing congestion of the area and so hampering healing, anti-inflammatory and pain-killing drugs will probably be given, and carefully applied supportive bandages to help control swelling and immobilize the part to restrict further injury. Cold packs may be advised.

- After this time, physiotherapy can begin, but much depends on the nature and severity of the injury. Physiotherapy is at least partly aimed at restoring the normal tissue structure and achieving better healing than if the injury were left to itself. Healing involves the production of 'scar tissue', which is weaker than the original, and not structurally organized in the same way. Tissues that should be separate and slide over each other can become joined by this scar tissue (then called adhesions because they adhere to each other); when work resumes, this tissue tears and re-injures the part.

• Laser or ultrasound (below) help to organize the tissue correctly, and careful leading in hand helps prevent

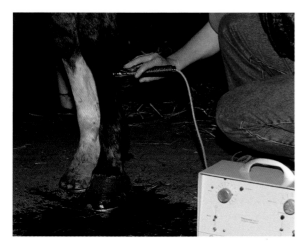

adhesions forming, making for a more effective repair. Sometimes with modern treatment and therapy the repair is so good that horses can return to their previous level of work. However, if the repair is not so good, that level of work will over-stress the part, and the injury will happen again.

• Over the years of an active horse's life, repeated injuries may occur to the same part, usually one or more legs, which ultimately means that the horse can do less and less demanding work. This is why very athletic horses such as racehorses, jumpers and eventers may retire to sports such as dressage and showing, or pursuits such as hacking and pleasure rides.

The outlook

If injuries are treated promptly and correctly, there is every chance that an excellent repair will take place, depending on the individual and the nature of his injury. Veterinary treatment, physiotherapy, complementary therapies and good management can all play their part in the healing process, and in the maintenance of the horse's future active life or comfortable retirement when the time comes.

93 Make use of herbalism and homoeopathy

Herbalism is probably the oldest therapy in the world, and homoeopathy is also very ancient in its earliest form. The two therapies are often confused, but they are different. Both, however, aim to correct the body's energies and stimulate the immune system to enable the patient's own resources to counteract the disease afflicting him or her.

Herbalism

Animals that lead a fairly free life seem to have retained a primitive ability to self-medicate, a nutritional intuition regarding the nutrients they need at a particular time. Humans may no longer be so good at this, and we often eat what we feel like -- to our detriment!

Because herbs are plants and eaten naturally by horses, it may be hard to regard them as medicinal: but the science of herbalism is definitely medicine. It can provide the body with nutrients to stimulate its immune system and/or to clear its energy channels, allowing energy to flow unimpeded, and to clear unwanted substances from the body.

It is used for both psychological and physical problems, whether acute or chronic, and although its two most popular uses in the horse world at present seem to be for calming horses down and helping to relieve the symptoms of arthritis, it can be used for almost any condition you can think of.

Although herbal feed supplements are available from tack stores and feed merchants, it is advisable to seek advice from a qualified herbalist at the manufacturer, or to consult a member of the National Institute of Medical Herbalists on veterinary referral.

Homoeopathy

This therapy is one of the hardest for orthodox vets to fully appreciate, even though there are fully trained and qualified homoeopathic veterinary surgeons. Homoeopathy treats the patient rather than the disease. A very detailed consultation is first made taking details of the patient's temperament, constitution, propensities, life history and present lifestyle. The aim is then to prescribe a remedy (which may come from an animal, vegetable or mineral source) to suit that mixture of qualities, and again, to encourage the body's energy to flow freely, and to help it to heal itself.

The principles of homoeopathy are that the symptoms caused by an overdose of a substance in a healthy being are the symptoms that can be cured by a small dose of that substance in a being that is sick. Symptoms of illness, whether psychological or physical, are regarded as expressions of disharmony and imbalance, therefore the patient is treated according to his or her individual traits in order to restore balance and energy flow. Therefore, two horses with the same condition may be given different remedies, but there are generally applicable remedies that can be used on a first aid basis, such as the well known arnica for pain and bruising.

For best results, consult a homoeopathic vet or a homoeopath on referral by your orthodox vet.

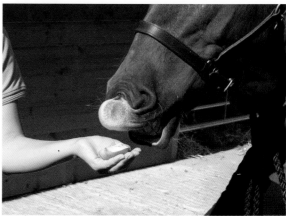

94 Employ manipulative therapies in health maintenance

Hands-on touch therapies have been used in health maintenance and in treating injuries for thousands of years. Massage originated in China and has been expanded upon since, and some other physical therapies stem from it. There is no doubt that they can all be very helpful, but it is important to use a trained, qualified therapist.

What's the difference between therapists?

Osteopaths and chiropractors work by adjusting and, where appropriate, readjusting the alignment of the skeleton, its muscles and joints. Chiropractors concentrate on the spine, whereas osteopaths may manipulate any skeletal part. Their purpose is to resolve painful conditions caused by misalignment of the skeleton, and so their work has a beneficial effect on the whole body, the nervous system and general health.

Physiotherapists have several techniques in their armoury. These may include:

- massage;
- manipulation;
- machines producing light waves or sound waves to work on tissues at different depths within tissues;
- exercise, and the use of hot and cold applications. The end result is hoped to be a faster and more effective healing process.

Massage concentrates mainly on soft tissues, with various moves involving light or heavier pressure, aimed partly at relieving muscle spasm and aligning muscle fibres. Masseurs may perform stretches, flexions and rotations aimed at loosening up and suppling both soft tissues and joints in order to increase their range of motion and enhance circulation, enabling it to move freely through the area.

Which therapy is best?

Every therapy mentioned can be excellent when performed by trained, qualified practitioners. Much depends on the nature of the condition being treated, and in the UK no physical therapist can work on your horse without referral from a veterinary surgeon – and most forward-thinking vets appreciate the benefits of these therapies. The field of equine 'bodywork' is becoming increasingly popular, and most high-level competition horses enjoy the services of a physical therapist in their training and maintenance regimes. But most working horses are athletes at their own level, and could benefit from these therapies, as appropriate.

THE BENEFITS OF SHIATSU

Shiatsu concentrates mainly on balancing the body's energy flow by enabling it to run freely through defined energy meridians or channels. It is closely related to acupuncture, but uses only pressure mainly from the fingertips – no needles. It also uses many acupressure points on the body, again aimed at adjusting its energy flow. Specific stretches and rotations may be used, aimed at suppling the body and working on parts of meridians too deep within it to be reached by external pressure. Shiatsu is used for psychological, emotional and physical conditions, for correcting disorders, but also for the maintenance of good health.

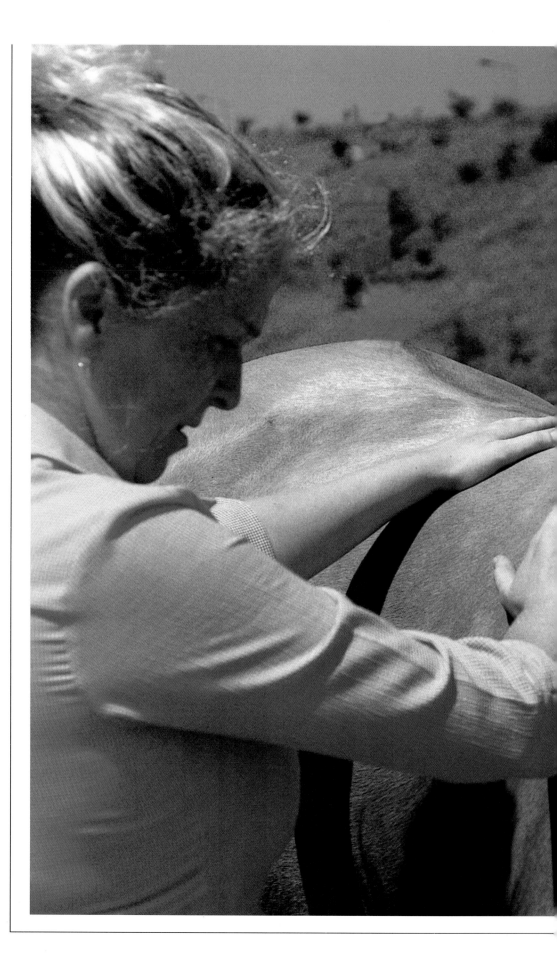

Holistic health

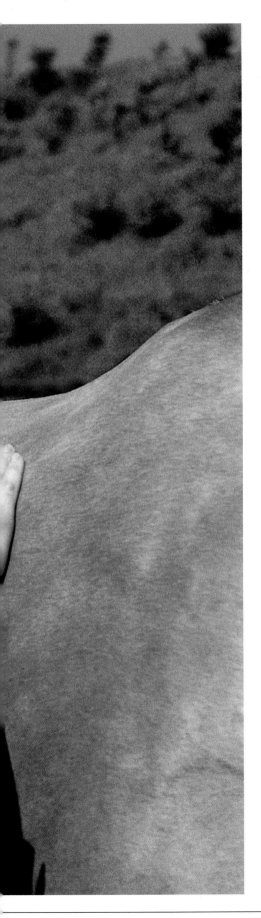

A healthy horse the holistic way

Several complementary therapies have already been mentioned – homoeopathy, acupuncture, herbalism – but this final section considers another four – aromatherapy, flower remedies, magnet therapy and healing – along with a couple of invaluable techniques, wisping and hand rubbing, that used to be standard practice in all the best run yards, but which have largely fallen out of use – to the detriment of horses and their well being.

There will certainly be people who run down anything with which they are not familiar, or which sounds improbable; and there will be some with an orthodox science background who may scoff at the more esoteric. Even major therapies such as herbalism, homoeopathy and acupuncture are denigrated by some people (even though certainly two of them are available to patients through the UK National Health Service, and all are funded for horses by some insurance companies), so they certainly wouldn't spare a passing glance at the final six therapies mentioned in this section. So, this book isn't for them: it's for those who are concerned about their horse's welfare, and who are sufficiently open-minded to consider anything that might help him to a healthier and happier life.

Finally, it is my real conviction that everyone, trained or otherwise, has the power to heal if they believe that it is possible, and have the will to do it. How many horses have you known flourish and thrive with a new owner who really cares? And sadly, how many deteriorate in health and performance with someone who doesn't? You never know what you can achieve till you try.

95 Try wisping to tone up the body system

Wisping is equivalent to giving a horse a massage and a muscular conditioning session after work and grooming. It is one of those traditional practices now done probably only in some of the best racing yards, but I was interested to see it recommended in the book *Essential Care of The Ridden Horse* by vet Peter Gray (David & Charles).

What is wisping?

Sometimes called banging and strapping, wisping is done with a hard pad made of hay (the wisp) on muscular areas

- to stimulate and supple them;
- to 'loosen' up any knots and spasms;
- to increase the circulation of blood, lymph and energy through them to enhance the delivery of oxygen and nutrients and the removal of toxins;
- to spread natural oils through the coat and over the skin.

How to make a wisp

Twist hay or haylage into a rope about your own height. To do this:

- twist a short length between your hands, then put one end of it under your foot and, keeping it taut, keep adding in hay as you twist.
- When the rope is finished, form two loops in the free end about the length of your hand (keeping your foot on the other end), and pass them alternately and tightly round the rope back and forth.
- At the top, tuck the short end that is left (from under your foot) under one of the turns, stamp on the wisp to firm and flatten it, and then damp it slightly.

The wisping technique

- Standing on, say, the left side of your horse, hold the wisp in your left hand (you can change over if/when you get tired) and bring it down on to the horse flat and with a moderate slap, leaning your weight into the horse. Draw the wisp down and back with the lie of the hair. The shaded areas on the illustration below indicate the areas to wisp.
- Give about six slaps or bangs in one place in a steady rhythm of about one per second, and then move on.
- Turn the wisp over when you change sides.

The idea is that the horse, once used to it, flinches his muscles in anticipation of the bang and leans into it, so working his body and muscles. The alternate compression and release of the muscle tissue massages it and stimulates circulation, and the whole process is physically and mentally relaxing and uplifting.

96 Use hand rubbing to massage, relax and tone

Hand rubbing is another traditional practice that horses enjoy; it, too, is a type of massage that presses and releases the muscles and other soft tissues (and the blood and lymph vessels they contain), encouraging circulation, comforting and relaxing the horse, and cleaning and/or drying his coat and putting a gloss on it.

Preparing both yourself and your horse

For yourself, it is better to wear a short-sleeved top, or to push your sleeves up to your elbows: then you can rub your horse with the flat of your hands and sometimes your forearms. You'll soon warm up on a cold day. For your horse, if the weather is cold, leave a rug unfastened and folded in half from front to back; you can move it backwards and forwards as you work. Groom the horse thoroughly, or brush him over to remove superficial dirt and dust if he is fairly clean. Hand rubbing a dirty horse just rubs the dirt into the coat and skin, and you will get filthy.

Hand-rubbing technique

- Start by talking to the horse as you just stroke the bottom of his neck and shoulders, using the flat of your hand with a firm but reassuring and confident pressure.
- When he gets the idea of what you are going to do, use both hands together and, working in the direction of the hair (except on the legs), lean your weight on your hands and forearms as you stroke and rub the horse all over from poll to tail.
- Go more gently on the throat, ribcage and belly, any bony parts and any areas where he feels sensitive.
- For the legs, squat down and clasp your fingers around each one, rubbing with the heels of your hands and palms upwards to help distribute blood and fluid up the limbs. If your horse is a kicker you may wish to leave out this part or to do only the forelegs, although regular, enjoyable handling such as this accustoms horses to contact.
- As you work on the forehand, lay the folded rug over his loins and quarters, bringing it forward over the neck and shoulders as you do the hind parts.
- When you change sides, put it back over the quarters, and start again from the poll.

97 Consult an aromatherapist

Working with scented essential oils is one of the most pleasurable and interesting therapies there is. The horse decides which oils he wants (needs), and seems to find the whole experience absorbing and emotionally satisfying. Oils can be used for emotional and physical disorders, and should be treated as medicines, not playthings.

How does aromatherapy work?

Few people would deny that smells have an effect on us, good or bad. Some scents attract us and make us feel wonderful, whilst others repel us and make us feel horrible. Animals generally have a much more sensitive sense of smell than humans. Horses are said to be able to smell others up to a mile away, and a stallion can smell precisely when a mare is amenable to mating.

The concentrated plant ('essential') oils used in aromatherapy contain fragrant molecules which, when they are breathed in and come into contact with the mucous membranes of the nose and other airways, dissolve in the moisture of the natural airway secretions and may pass into the blood and lymphatic systems. They can have an effect on the mental, emotional and physical condition of the horse. Massaged on the skin, some believe that they pass through it and are inhaled at the same time.

What conditions is it used for?

- When they are inhaled or massaged in, the oils can be used for many conditions including physical injuries, diarrhoea and constipation, osteoarthritis, stress relief, emotional issues and problems of temperament.
- When used under the supervision of a vet and/or trained aromatherapist, oils can be licked off the hand or dropped on to the tongue and then may be used for colic, urinary tract infections, breeding problems, internal soft tissue damage, infections, parasitic infestations and other skin conditions.

What can I do?

There are several good books available on the subject, but as usual, the best way is to first consult a professional aromatherapist on veterinary referral. He or she will come and take a history of your horse and his problem or normal state of being, and will ask him to try a few oils. Those the horse is interested in may be used individually or in a blend; those that he turns away from are not what he needs at that particular point.

The therapist will help you set up a basic kit and show you how to use it so that you acquire a reasonable working knowledge of the therapy, though it should be backed up by occasional consultations.

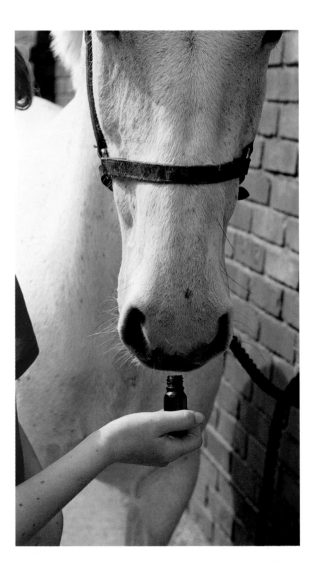

98 Correct mind and spirit with flower remedies

The most famous flower remedies are those devised by orthodox physician Dr Edward Bach, but there are others, not strictly homoeopathic remedies but they do work on similar principles. Dr Bach believed that flowers could treat excesses of personality traits, and mental attitudes that might progress to physical disorders.

How do flower remedies work?

- Like other complementary therapists (whether or not they also have orthodox training and qualifications), the practitioner treats the human or animal patient's body, mind and spirit, rather than the disorder: Dr Bach believed that by correcting the mind and spirit, the disease would not progress to physical manifestation. His research led him to find out which flowers could help which traits and attitudes, and he then developed the method of preparing the remedies from them.
- Flowerheads are gathered and left in a clear glass bowl in pure water and in strong sunlight so that the 'healing signature' of the flower is taken up by the water. The liquid is then filtered and preserved in equal parts of brandy as a preservative.
- Dropped into the horse's drinking water or inside his lips several times a day, the appropriate remedy is used until the trait or attitude improves, perhaps then being replaced by another.
- As the layers of emotion are 'stripped away', the remedy or blend is changed to treat any new excesses of emotion that have been brought to light, so over time even deep-seated problems can be improved.

What can I do?

Remedies and informative books and leaflets are available from chemists, health stores and similar outlets, and there are qualified therapists available to help assess the personality traits that may be causing problems in your horse. As with any therapy, it is usually best to start off with a professional assessment, but a good therapist will help you with occasional consultations to treat your own horse.

99 Benefit health through magnet therapy

It is an undisputed fact that the earth has a magnetic field that affects many aspects of life on this planet – yet some people find it hard to believe that magnetism has a direct effect on a living creature. Magnets have an electric charge, and so does every atom in the bodies of both ourselves and our horses – though it isn't certain just what their effect is.

So how is magnet therapy believed to work?

- Many enthusiasts of magnet therapy's benefits believe that it works by improving the ability of the blood to carry oxygen and iron (a metal that attracts magnets) in its haemoglobin, possibly by exciting the atoms in the iron.
- Because our bodies are composed of electrically charged atoms, it could be that placing a magnet near disrupted, injured tissue, or passing electrically pulsed magnetism through it, brings about a change or enhanced functioning in the atoms, which encourages healing.
- Another theory is that the unnatural amount of human-generated electricity in our environment has an adverse effect on the earth's own magnetism, and that by wearing magnets or undergoing pulsed electro-magnetic therapy we help to correct our bodies' magnetism, which in turn benefits our health and natural functioning.

What can I do?

- There are many magnetic products on the market for humans and animals. Horse magazines regularly carry advertisements for static magnetic products (not pulsed by electricity) such as pastern straps, neck straps and chains, knee pads, boots and rugs with magnetic inserts, and also for products –

usually rugs – that need an electric current to pulse the magnetism through injured areas.

- I would prefer to consult a physiotherapist before using electrically pulsed products, because this is one of the therapies used by them, according to circumstances. Then you would be sure that you were using the correct setting for your horse's problem, and you could also get expert advice on general safety aspects.
- Using static magnetic products does not harm a horse provided you watch for correct fit and any sign of rubbing, and do not leave the item on the horse permanently. For instance, most suppliers recommend

that their product is used, say, overnight or for several hours during the day.

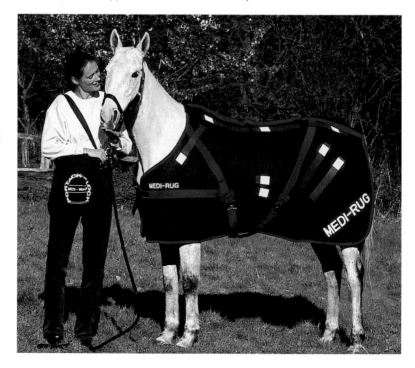

100 If distant healing works for you, then use it...

There are some therapies that defy if not the imagination then certainly reason and logic in attempting to define how they work. The three mentioned in this section come into that category – but all I can say is, that if something works for you and yours, then use it.

Radionics

Sometimes known as 'the (black) box', radionics is otherwise known as 'distant healing', and the distance can be thousands of miles. Practitioners use a 'witness' from the patient, such as a lock of hair, some horn or fingernail, a little piece of skin or a drop of blood, all of which are believed to contain the patient's energy pattern. By dowsing over the witness with a pendulum, they can assess disharmonies and imbalances, and send energy vibrations to the patient via the witness by means of radionic instruments that suggest to the tissues how to repair themselves. Apparently, just how the energy is transmitted still cannot be explained, but it does certainly appear to work.

Healing (by faith or spirituality)

There are some people who seem to have naturally 'healing hands', or even the ability to send healing to people or animals distant from them. Distant healers seem able to contact a person or animal they hear about, or to whom, or about whom they speak on the 'phone.

I think that the therapy may work simply by someone wishing sincerely to help and to 'send' healing by envisaging it surrounding the patient. Some people certainly seem to be better at healing than others, but I firmly believe we can all do it to some extent with concentration, goodwill and focus.

Reiki

Reiki seems to be a structured version of the above therapy, healing, with philosophical similarities to several Eastern therapies. The practitioner acts as a centre for the attraction and concentration of energy from the environment, which then passes to the patient. Reiki can, apparently, be sent from a distance, and can be applied to individuals, groups, nations or even the entire planet, I have been told.

It can also be used alone, or to complement any other kind of healing, acting as a supportive and strengthening force for good in psychological or physical distress or disorder. Students of Reiki are 'attuned' to, or initiated into it at different levels. The student must sincerely want to help and heal others, and I know of many people who believe in it.

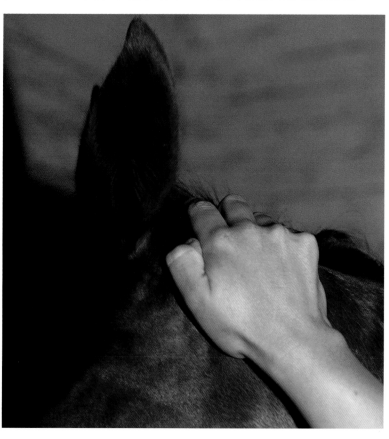

Useful addresses

UK

Association of Chartered Physiotherapists in Animal Therapy
Moorland House
Salter's Lane
Winchester
Hants.
SO22 5JP
Tel: (01962) 863801

Association of Master Saddlers
Kettles Farm
Mickfield
Stowmarket
Suffolk
IP14 6BY
Tel: (01499) 711642

British Association of Equine Dental Technicians
The Bungalow
Bonehill Road
Mile Oak
Tamworth
Staffordshire
B78 3PS
Tel: (01827) 284718

British Association of Holistic Nutrition and Medicine
Borough Court
Hartley Wintney
Basingstoke
Hants.
RG27 8JA
Tel: (01252) 843282

British Association of Homoeopathic Veterinary Surgeons
Chinham House
Stanford-in-the-Vale
Faringdon
Oxfordshire
SN7 8NQ
Tel: (01367) 710324

British Equestrian Trade Association
Stockeld Park
Wetherby
West Yorkshire
LS22 4AW
Tel: (01937) 582111

The British Herbal Medicine Association
1 Wickham Road
Bournemouth
Dorset
BH7 6JX

British Osteopathic Association
Langham House, Mill Street
Luton
Bedfordshire
LU1 2NA
Tel: (01582) 488455

British Veterinary Acupuncture Association
East Park Cottage
Handcross
West Sussex
RH17 6BD
Tel: (01444) 400213

The Classical Riding Club
Eden Hall
Kelso
Roxburghshire
Scotland
TD5 7QD
Fax: (01890) 830667

The Dr Edward Bach Centre
Mount Vernon
Sotwell
Wallingford
Oxon
OX10 0PX

Equine Aromatherapy Association
PO Box 19, Hay-on-Wye
Hereford
HR3 5AE

Equine Behaviour Forum Grove Cottage
Brinkley
Newmarket
Suffolk
CB8 0SF
Tel: (01223) 836970

The Equine Shiatsu Association
Membership Secretary
Jill Blake tESA(P)
St. Peters Stud
Upper Beeding
West Sussex
BN44 3HP
Tel: (01903) 814860

Equine Sports Massage Association
17 Gloucester Road
Stratton
Cirencester
Glos
GL7 2LB
Tel: (01285) 650275

Farriers Registration Council
Sefton House, Adam Court
Newark Road
Peterborough
Tel: (01733) 319911

McTimoney Chiropractic Association
21 High Street
Eynsham
Oxford
OX8 1HE
Tel: (018650) 880974

National Federation of Spiritual Healers
Old Manor Farm Studio
Church Street
Sunbury-on-Thames
Middlesex
TW16 6RG

The Radionic Association
Berlein House
Goose Green
Deddington
Banbury
Oxon OX15 0SZ
Tel: (01869) 338852

TTEAM – Tellington Touch Equine Awareness Method
TTEAM Centre
Tilley Farm
Farmborough
Bath BA2 0AB
Tel: (01761) 471128
www.ttouchtteam.co.uk

Intelligent Horsemanship
Lethornes
Lambourn
Hungerford
Berkshire
RG17 8QS
Tel: (01488) 71300

National Sweet Itch Helpline
Rhos Uchaf
LLanfynydd
Nr Wrexham
Flintshire
LL11 5HR
Tel: (01352) 771718

Goldson Horsewear
Lower Lamborne Farm
Tolcarne Hill
St Day
Redruth
TR16 5HA
Tel: (01209) 821612

The Laminitis Clinic
Mead House Farm
Dauntsey
Chippenham
Wiltshire
SN15 4JA
Tel: 0905 105 105 1
(Note: calls are charged at £1.00 per minute)
www.laminitis.org

NORTH AMERICA

American Association of Equine Practitioners
4075 Iron Works Parkway
Lexington, KY 40511

American Farrier's Association
4059 Iron Works Parkway,
Suite 1
Lexington, KY 40511

American Medical Equestrian Association
PO Box 130848
Birmingham
AL 35213–0848

American Veterinary Chiropractic Association
442154 E 140 Rd
Bluejacket
Oklahoma 74333

American Veterinary Medical Association
1931 North Meacham Road
Suite 100
Schaumburg
IL 60173

TTEAM US Office
PO Box 3793
Sante Fé
New Mexico 87501-3793

AUSTRALIA

Australian Veterinary Association
PO Box 371
Artarmon
NSW 1570

NEW ZEALAND

New Zealand Veterinary Association Inc.
PO Box 11-212
Manners Street
Wellington

Index

PICTURE ACKNOWLEDGEMENTS

All photography by David Waters and Dan Tucker at Horsepix.co.uk except pages listed below.
    With its roots in horse country and staffed by horse people, Horsepix is a leading provider of high quality equestrian stock photography.

David & Charles/Andy Perkins: p11(left)
David & Charles/Bob Atkins: p17
David & Charles/Neil Hepworth: p25

Jackson Arenas: p47
David & Charles/Kit Houghton: pp 80, 81, 112
David & Charles/Bob Langrish: pp 121, 149
Karen Coumbe: p132
Kit Houghton: pp 127, 138, 139
David & Charles/Susan McBane: pp 141, 142–3
Magno-Pulse Ltd: p148

Illustrations on p90 by Dianne Breeze
Illustrations on pp 103, 144 by Maggie Raynor
Illustrations on pp 118, 119 by Ethan Danielson